Loss And Growth:

The Grief Spiral

Transformative Bereavement

Elissa Bishop-Becker,
M.Ed., LPC, NCC

The New
Atlantian Library

The New Atlantian Library is an imprint of
ABSOLUTELY AMAZING eBOOKS

Published by Whiz Bang LLC, 926 Truman Avenue, Key West, Florida 33040, USA

This work is based on factual events. While the author has made every effort to provide accurate information at the time of publication, neither the publisher nor the author assumes any responsibility for errors, or for changes that occur after publication. Further, the publisher does not have any control over and does not assume any responsibility for author or third-party websites or their contents.

For information contact
Publisher@AbsolutelyAmazingEbooks.com
ISBN-13: 978-0615892283
ISBN-10: 0615892280

To my beloved Ericka, who leads the way, and whose abundant love, laughter, energy, and hair have informed my life. You taught me to live, to enjoy, to learn, and to remember. I carry your heart.

Preface

Feeling as if I were in some awful nightmare, I walked into the hospital with my husband Randy. The police met us outside the door, and one of the officers asked us to follow him. I kept asking about Ericka, but no one would say anything. I walked right past the drunk driver who had killed her and our eyes met, but I didn't know then who he was. The officer took us down the hall and into a private room. I knew something was terribly wrong. Then he told us about the accident and when I asked about Ericka, he just looked at me sorrowfully and shook his head. "She didn't make it," he said. I screamed, "NO! NO! NO!" and kicked the metal hospital bed frame as hard as I could, as if that would ground me or make the world make sense again.

The unthinkable, the unimaginable, the unbearable had happened. My life as I knew it died with my child.

I wrote those words about my own experience on August 20, 1995, when I learned of the death of my 20-year-old daughter in a collision with a drunk driver who was driving his pickup truck in the wrong direction on I-64 near Williamsburg, Virginia. My own grief journey began with the loss of my only child.

We had moved to Williamsburg 2 weeks earlier. Ericka had spent the summer as a resident counselor in the Yale Summer Program. She traveled from New Haven by train to be with us in her new home before beginning her junior year. Her stepsister Lee was to join her at Yale as a freshman the following week. My husband Randy was about to begin his new ministry with the Williamsburg Unitarian Universalists. His younger daughter Suki was coming from Long Island to live with us and start high school. Our lives seemed full of promise, and when Ericka's ended none of us could imagine how they could continue. And the truth was that they could not continue – not as they had been.

The 3 years following Ericka's death were filled with pain, chaos, self-discovery, awe, and hope. In the Fall of 1998, I enrolled in the College of William and Mary as a student in the Master's program in Community Counseling. Through that intense and enlightening experience I found the new direction that brought me fulfillment and made meaning of my loss. Although there were no courses in death, dying, or grief in the program, I was able to focus my research and internship experiences on grief and grief counseling. I slowly evolved my own approach, and as my clients responded and found new meaning and direction for their own lives I began to realize I had something important to share with others in the counseling field, and with my larger community.

This was made even clearer to me when I did post-graduate counseling in the college addictions clinic and learned that I could apply my budding theory to issues as seemingly diverse as addictions, codependency, and sexual abuse. I gradually became aware that the grief process is the change process – and counseling, of course, is all about change. Life, I came to understand, is a process of dealing with loss. And those who deal well with loss deal well with life.

The theory presented in this book is that which guided me through the grief process. It evolved in a series of infinitely small steps as I learned to live after a loss that I never imagined I could survive. I realize now that if I had tried to remain the same – tried to resume my life as it had been before Ericka's death – I would have found only pain and emptiness, for nothing can be built on what no longer exists. By accepting my loss, accepting the ways I had changed and forming a new identity in the wake of that loss, finding a new way to continue in relationship with Ericka by discovering what was essential about the relationship we had, and moving forward into the future with that relationship as a foundation for the creation of new experiences, I slowly revealed to myself a new identity and a new world that I could live in with meaning and purpose. So, not only have I changed through this process, but so has my perception of the world I inhabit.

This process was not easy. The grief process takes much energy and focus and hope. There were many times I wanted to give up, many times I questioned whether all the effort was worthwhile, and many times I felt inadequate to continue. When Ericka died, all I thought about was her until I realized that my life was not just a waiting room to see her; and that I had things to do and learn in this life. I had no sense of how to focus my scattered energy until I learned to stop trying to get others to energize me, to deal with my feelings of guilt and fear, let go of the illusion of control, and learn how to create my own energy by being who I am. I focused on Ericka's life and what she had given me and what was gone until I learned to accept myself, ask "What's in the glass," and start my life all over again by focusing on what I could offer and receive. I learned to deal with change by learning to recognize that pain is a signal that says "Don't stop the process now, there's more to come that will bring joy and fulfillment and balance." I began to think non-linearly-looking at time as sequence and focusing forward to take infinitely small steps toward a meaningful future while sorting out what I could keep of the past. I learned that you cannot dance if you're standing still. But probably what has helped me the most is the ability to see crisis as opportunity, and to stay open to whatever comes, with hope that on the other side of the pain lies transformation and laughter and eternal love. And in my dreams of the future, I see a graceful Ericka greeting me with outstretched arms, saying "You done good, Mom, let's go dancing."

-EBB

*Note on How to Use this Book

The Epilogue contains a lot of background information on how grief is perceived in our culture, and how that perception is changing from the medical model to the transformative model. If you are a counselor, teacher, researcher, or simply interested in the shoulders that my theory stands on, you will probably find it valuable to read. If you are grieving and are only interested in how my theory can help you recover from your loss and discover the life that waits for you in a future that you cannot yet see, you can skip the Epilogue without missing anything you need to know. Of course, you can always read it if your curiosity gets the better of you!

The exercises, techniques, and resources presented throughout the book and in the appendices are tools that everyone can use.

Whether or not you are a professional, I suggest that you take the information presented here slowly and in bite-sized pieces, giving yourself time to ponder and digest.

Acknowledgments

So many people have helped me get to this point that it seems a daunting task to thank them all, but I will try and hope anyone I have inadvertently left out will know that their contribution is part of the process that created my new life, and this book.

First, Ericka, who transformed my life and showed me the horizon; Papa, who died 3 months after Ericka, but not before teaching me to love words and ideas; my husband the Rev. Dr. Randolph Becker, who loved, learned from, and taught me, and who believed in the value of the sometimes mystifying twists and turns my grief process took; Lee, who shared my grief and allowed me to be a mom to her after I lost my only child; Suki, who moved to Virginia to live with me and Randy; the Williamsburg Unitarian Universalists, who supported and hugged me as I cried every Sunday in church for the first year; Ericka's friends, too many to name individually (but I must mention Lizzie-Pooh, Ali, Michelle, and Niki), who have continued contact with me and helped me feel her continuing presence in their hearts and developing journeys; Yale University, especially Dr. Stanton and Marcia Wheeler, true friends who helped us create Ericka's Phone Card and Ericka's Room in Morse College; Joan Windsor, my counselor who helped me grow spiritually and emotionally after Ericka's death when I could not see anything ahead in the darkness; Martha Petit, my hospice internship supervisor, who gave me the freedom to evolve my counseling approach, and did it with love and laughter; the professors in the Community Counseling program at the College of William and Mary: Dr. Charles (Rick) Gressard, who understood I had something valuable to contribute to the addictions clinic and let me; Laurie Rokutani, Dr. Charles (Rip) McAdams, Dr. Victoria Foster, Dr. Charles (Chas) Matthews, Dr. Norma Day-Vines, and Dr. George Bass, all of whom supported my interest in grief counseling and research; my student cohort at the College, who became friends and taught me that stress can be fun; the board members who joined me in creating the Center for Transformative Counseling: Martha Petit, Randy Becker, Rick Gressard, John Rajniak, Barb Kaplan, Beulah Davis, and Kathryn O'Neil; everyone along the way – clients, friends, and acquaintances – who opened their lives to me and gave me the privilege of using what I have learned to help them; all those who allowed me to include their stories in this book; and my beautiful, fluffy, golden kitty Mufi, who cuddled with me at night and gave me unconditional love when that was exactly what I needed.

The stories in this book come from my clients, friends, and contacts made through the Internet. Many of them are composites. I have changed the names and, in some cases, personal details, but never the essence or meaning.

Enough about me. Now about the process of recovery from grief.

CONTENTS

Preface
Acknowledgments

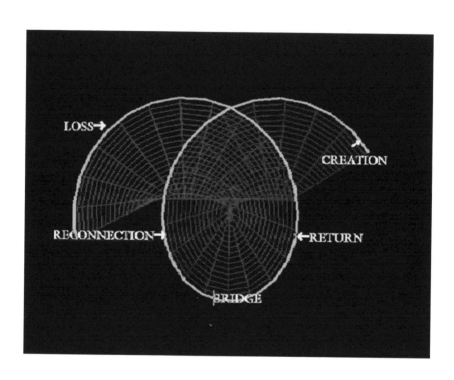

Stage 1: Loss

Stop all the clocks, cut off the telephone,
Prevent the dog from barking with a juicy bone.
Silence the pianos and with muffled drum
Bring out the coffin, let the mourners come.

-WH Auden (from *Funeral Blues*)

Chapter 1
Loss

Loss: The unthinkable, the unimaginable, the unbearable. We are never prepared for it, no matter how far in advance we know it will happen – such as with a terminal illness – and no matter how many previous losses we have experienced. Each loss is unique and has its own meaning to each individual involved. One cannot know how another feels about a particular loss, but we can help and support each other by using what we have learned from our own experience. Loss is a universal human experience, and as tempting as it may be to try to minimize or maintain the illusion of control over it, we diminish our own humanity when we do not deal with the challenges and lessons it presents.

Elisabeth Kübler-Ross – the pioneering psychiatrist whose experience with and theory of death and dying broke through a wall that Western society had carefully constructed between itself and end-of-life issues – wrote that it is impossible for us to conceive of our own death, but as we learn to deal with loss we can come to a new relationship with life that enables us to accept death as part of living. She outlined her now-famous 5 stages of death and dying, which were subsequently generalized to apply to the grief process (Kübler-Ross, 1969). Her 5 stages of Denial, Anger, Bargaining, Depression, and Acceptance comprise what I see as the first stage of bereavement: Loss.

As I explain in the Epilogue, the process of change is a spiral rather than a straight line leading directly from Point A to Point B. This first stage of Loss is the initial forward direction of a line as it moves into becoming a spiral.

Chapter 2
Denial

The nearly universal response upon hearing about the death of a loved one is: "No!" It makes no sense within the context of the world as we know it, and so we deny its reality to protect ourselves from the life-threatening shock of the event. We try to keep things the same, which takes an enormous amount of energy.

Emma was 31 when her son drowned at the age of 11. "The police came to my door," she said 14 months later. "This experience haunts me to this day. That feeling when the words leave their lips, it's like everything is in slow motion and you get that feeling right through your system. You then realize what they have said, and it hits you like a train going a million miles an hour. My legs gave way at that point and I screamed at the top of my lungs NO NO NO NO NO NO. I was alone in the house when the police came. When they told me I crawled across the floor like a baby, just screaming. I had to get to the phone and tell everyone. I truly thought I was going to have a heart attack that night, my heart was pounding so hard and my crying was causing me to hyperventilate. I will never forget the look on one of the cop's faces. He was as white as anything and he couldn't look me in the face. I ended up punching the cop that told me my son was dead and wasn't coming home to me. Shock does some terrible things to you."

Most of us experience a sense of unreality, as though we were walking around in a fog that buffers us from the world and softens our sharp, unrelenting focus on a loss that seems too fundamentally painful to accept. Our sense of time is different – a month seems to whiz by, while hours can feel endless. Memories of the past appear with vivid clarity, while the present seems muffled and distant. We typically feel off-balance, disoriented, fearful, and often as though life itself had abandoned us – had broken its promise of the present and future. Despair and hopelessness are also feelings that arise during this very vulnerable phase.

George was 38 years old when he came to see me just 2 weeks after his mother's death. His mom died a year – almost to the day – after his father. Both of his parents died from cancer. He was an only child. He never married, and had no children. He and his parents were very close, did a lot together and he called his mom his "best friend."

George said he was feeling numb. Because his dad was not emotionally expressive, he was concerned about his own ability to feel his feelings. He wanted to cry but could not, and was sleeping fitfully. He was feeling overwhelmed with things needing to be taken care of, and concerned with what others thought about how he was handling them. He had unresolved issues with his dad's death because his mom's illness had prevented him from grieving then – feeling he needed to protect her. He seemed restless – an indication of separation anxiety. During our fourth session he remarked that he was surprised by how much time had passed since his mom's death.

This is a step characterized by a sense of numbness. Because of the self-protective layer of denial, we are often surprised at how well we seem to be coping with the loss. Some grievers express amazement that they have survived what they had previously considered too painful to bear. Especially when the loss was not sudden or traumatic, some remark that they expected to feel worse than they do. They feel stronger and more in control than they expected, and may say things like, "I'm ok. I'm really doing fine, so don't worry about me." Others around them will say things like, "I'm glad to see you're not devastated by this," or

"You must be strong. You're handling all of this so well." Problems develop at this step when we receive so much social approval for our apparent strength that we allow ourselves to get stuck and do not seek help when we need it.

This phase is the psychic equivalent to being physically wounded. When we receive a physical wound, we are protected by the shock of it from feeling unbearable pain. It is only when the healing begins that we begin to feel the pain of the wound.

Anna was 39 when her daughter Laura died from epilepsy at the age of 17. Two and a half months after Laura's death Anna said, "I am aware that, while I may be going fine now, I do fear that one of these days things may come screeching to a halt for me. I may wake up or come out of this daze and find it has all fallen apart and that I can't cope. I fear ending up in a rubber room.

"I hear every day from friends and colleagues, 'You're taking this all so well, such a strong lady.' Funny, I don't feel strong. My mom and dad both have commented on how strong I've been. Even a couple of my sisters-in-law have said so. Sometimes I just want to crawl in a hole and hide there and cry and wallow in it! But I am somehow able to live up to the expectations and responsibilities I have taken on. I fear that one day I may not be able to,

and everyone will wonder what has happened to me. I fear letting others down – so see, I have my hang-ups.

"I'm kind of up and down. As long as I stay busy, I'm ok, for the most part. I've learned that when I take control of situations myself, I do better. But when I lay down at night . . . WHAM! the darkness creeps in around me and it hits like a Mack truck. I end up crying and aching and not sleeping. Not a day goes by, hardly, that I don't wish: O please, God, let me wake up and find it isn't so!"

This is the time when, in general, grievers have the greatest amount of support. The casserole brigade appears. Family, friends, and community rally around and reinforce that protective buffer between the real world and us. Grievers often express the need to take care of others. We are acutely aware of the discomfort and fear that others feel in our presence. We focus on others and on maintaining a distance from our new reality, which is shrouded in the mists of an unknown and often terrifying future.

Thomas was a 62-year-old retired minister who came to the hospice bereavement group about a month after his wife's death from cancer. Shortly before his wife was diagnosed, they had built their "dream house" and made plans to travel and spend more time together. Now he felt confused and disoriented, questioning what it was all for and feeling acutely the loss of what was supposed to be their blissful future.

Thomas had been, he thought, prepared for his wife's death and had a lot of support from members of his family and congregation. As is the experience of many widowers, he received attention and nurturing from female acquaintances. When he was alone he cried easily, and was satisfied that he could feel his feelings. But he was sensitive to those around him and tried to put them at ease – to minister to them as he had always done when that was his professional role.

The danger inherent in the outpouring of love, sympathy, attention, and support that some of us experience is that we might learn to avoid our pain by allowing others to maintain the protective buffer indefinitely. Thomas did not, but some do get stuck at this point – or shortly following this point – and become what counselors sadly call "professional grievers." These are those who have so little faith in their own strength to survive the grief process, have had so little prior experience that has tested them, or are so terrified of life, that they learn to manipulate others so that they can stand still and never move forward.

Sarah was a 53-year-old college professor whose husband died suddenly from a heart attack. Sarah was traumatized and could not deal with the overwhelming intensity of her feelings. She had always been an intellectual and focused on control, and she tried to use her reason to cope with this loss. She mapped out a "logical" recovery plan for herself, thinking that what she needed to do was just "tough it out." "Life goes on," she said. When I suggested to her that our support group might be helpful, she looked me straight in the eye and said, "I will not be attending." What I saw behind the defiance in her eyes was fear.

Over time it became clear that Sarah was not moving forward. Her life was no different than it had been at the time of her husband's death, she cried with the same moderate intensity of emotion – as if measuring out her tears and feelings – told the same stories about their life together, and maintained the same relationships in the same way. She turned increasingly to alcohol to numb her pain, and she became a rescuer – dependent on others she felt she could help – to give her a sense of her own identity and self-worth.

Hannah's son had died 2 months earlier in an auto accident. She said, "Our old life has died, and was buried with Toki, and the changes are so hard to cope with.

Missing my son, missing the old life I had, missing the joy that used to be ours. I am living a life that does not feel like it belongs to me yet. I hope one day it will feel less strange and totally weird. I feel to a degree unattached to the life I live now.

"It terrifies me this terrible hurt inside, and living with it forever is enough to make one want to quit living already. I hope one day the pain will be less intense. I am running from it for now, because it is like a giant beast chasing after me. I have had many say, one day I must face the beast to heal it. But it is so much larger and more scary than I ever thought possible. So for now I run, and I hope I survive and learn to live with this. I must believe there is hope to escape this grieving beast that hangs about our house."

In the normal course of the grief process the protection of shock serves us well when we need to deal with the details of such things as wills, funerals, wakes, insurance policies, obituaries, etc. Even though concentration is difficult, and memory and judgment are clouded, as long as material concerns take precedence there is something of the past to hold onto – and that can feel both reassuring and impossibly painful at a time when very little appears clear cut, and when the noise of *why* questions constantly swirl, seemingly uncontrollably, in our minds.

Part of the attempt to hold onto the past is replaying the events of and around the death. Grievers often report constant intrusive thoughts about the event, which I believe serve two primary purposes: 1. To help us teach ourselves that the event is real, and 2. As a grounding, or focal point, when our world has been severely disrupted and is out of balance. Journaling can be very helpful, making the thoughts concrete; and telling the story over and over to anyone who will listen is a healing and necessary part of the process. Those who are newly bereaved are usually very appreciative of those who have the patience to listen to their story. In counseling, I have found that one of the ways to monitor progress is to track changes in the story and the way it is related. To think that hearing it once is enough is to mistake content for process.

There is no time limit to any part of the grief process, and the shock – especially in the case of trauma or the loss of a child, which by definition is traumatic – can be prolonged when the appropriate help is not sought or available.

Martha was 56. Her daughter, Jessica, had died suddenly of an aneurysm 5 months before we met. Jessica was 30 years old, Martha's "best friend" and her "baby." Martha had not been able to say the words "dead" or "death" in connection with Jessica. She repeated the story of Jessica's death over and over again.

During the first few months of our sessions, Martha kept saying "I can't believe she's gone. It's so hard. It hurts so bad. It's like I've got her things waiting for her to come back, but I know she's not going to come back." Martha also talked about not being able to concentrate or remember "little stuff." Shopping, traveling, looking at photos, and other activities she associated with Jessica evoked enormous anxiety. She dreamed about her son dying, afraid of losing another child.

The presence of others is distracting, and many of us find that when we are not alone our pain diminishes. The protective numbness is not absolute, and unbearable pain often pierces our protective emotional shield. Many of us find that being alone intensifies our pain – there are no distractions, and we feel unsafe. There is often a sense that, "If this could happen, then anything could happen," a feeling of walking on quicksand, and a tendency to anticipate the next loss and to wait for "the other shoe to drop."

Sophie was 43 when her mother died of cancer while visiting in Sophie's home. Sophie had always looked outside herself for support and – like her mother –

focused on taking care of others' needs. Her family was the center of her universe. She said she was afraid of what might happen, afraid of being alone. She felt unsafe and, even though it was exhausting her, felt she needed to protect her family and watch them constantly.

Amy, 34, lost her baby when she was 19. He had died minutes after he was born. She had nightmares in which she saw a dead little boy, and she woke up feeling "anxious, scared, and worried that something would happen to Daniel" (her youngest stepson). When her husband was away on business she had to sleep with all the lights and the TV on because she felt unsafe and imagined someone was breaking into her house.

Amy was still an adolescent when she lost her baby. The uncertainty and self-consciousness of adolescents often leads to their suppression or repression of subjective responses. The adolescent struggling to maintain control may not have any immediately visible reaction to a loss at all. Often the extreme stress they experience goes unnoticed because others are in shock and tend to focus on those whose expressions of grief are more overt. Their grief is often misperceived as a developmental problem or as acting out. Male adolescents may initially react with aggressive antisocial behavior; many have been incarcerated following a traumatic loss. And females may initially react with self-injurious behavior, including sexual promiscuity.

Chloe, a 41-year-old Japanese-American, lost her father at the age of 14. "I was Daddy's little girl," she said. She had been taught by her Japanese mother to be "a good girl," and she was shy and passive. Having learned that it was unacceptable to express her emotions, she acted out. She began to argue with and rebel against her mom, and her grades dropped after she had been a good student all her life. She became promiscuous, had a brief one-sided relationship with an older man, got pregnant, and had an abortion without telling anyone. Terrified that her mother would totally reject her, she handled all the arrangements for the abortion herself and has kept it a secret to this day. Afterwards she married an emotionally abusive man and, while still married to him, had a series of sexual relationships. None of her relationships were satisfying, but she clung to each one desperately for fear of being abandoned again. "Each one feels like my last chance," she said.

Many grievers receive medication or begin to self-medicate at this point in the process. Over-medication immediately following a death can prevent us from fully experiencing or even remembering rituals and funeral preparations, participation in which are essential to an uncomplicated grief process. When a child has died, the parents may feel guilty "over the lack of appropriate 'feelings' which they should have experienced . . . Overuse of drugs can produce the same severe emotional illness they are designed to prevent" (Patterson, 1972).

Amy's son's cause of death was officially recorded as "unknown." Her family refused to talk about it at all. Traumatized and without support, she self-medicated to cope with the pain – which started a chain reaction of events that led to the dissolution of her marriage, the loss to adoption of her older child, and her attempted suicide. Sixteen years later she talked about feeling the pain, "like it was yesterday. I can see everything that happened like I was watching TV. I felt nothing when I saw him at the funeral. It wasn't real. I plugged my ears and shut my eyes. I just wanted to go home. Why didn't I hold him? I couldn't tell you if he was warm or cold. I am tired of going back and reliving this. I thought time was supposed to make it better."

In addition to the substances that can lead to physical addiction, we may become addicted to anything that helps us fill the void left by the loss. Buying things is often used for this purpose; "retail therapy" can be a quick fix that is as addictive as any substance.

Anna said, "I suddenly realized that I had not paid several very important bills. I frantically started calling up these companies and begging for forgiveness and time. Not only did I not pay bills, I compensated for my feelings of loss by going shopping and buying things (clothes, eating out because I didn't feel like cooking or cleaning) that I shouldn't have. It made me feel better at the time, but I'm paying for it now."

It is during this phase that many of us realize for the first time – because we are finally forced to focus on what nearly everyone fears acknowledging – that the experience of loss is universal. People who have experienced similar losses will tell us their stories, and we often become fascinated with reading the information on gravestones and in obituaries. We begin to teach ourselves that we are not alone, but participate in a universe that is seemingly arbitrary, unpredictable, painful, and frightening. The world is no longer black and white, but a confusing mixture of colors and shades – many of which we see as though for the first time.

Griever's Toolbox:

★ Tell the story in as much detail as possible (over and over again).

★ Familiarize yourself with the Common Symptoms and Feelings of Grief (see Appendix A)

★ Keep a journal and a dream journal (see Appendix A).

★ Be aware of medication/self-medication issues. Also be aware of a tendency toward other addictions (e.g., shopping, constant activity, food, etc.).

★ Be mindful of physical self-care, and monitor eating and sleeping problems and illnesses.

★ Understand that grief feels worse before it gets better. As when someone is physically wounded, the shock protects you from the pain until you can deal with it.

★ Learn about what to expect in the next stages (depending on how much you want to know)

★ Focus on your strengths and ability to survive.

★ Unless unavoidable, do not make major life-changing decisions for at least one year.

★ Focus on small, concrete, physical tasks that are grounding (e.g., knitting, woodworking, jigsaw puzzles, painting, cooking, washing, cleaning, gardening, etc.)

★ Create a ritual or memorial, especially if you have not participated in a funeral or other ceremony (see Appendix A).

★ Self-educate about the universality of loss by visiting

cemeteries, speaking to other grievers and hearing their stories, reading, and watching movies dealing with loss (see Appendix A).

★ Read How to Help (Appendix A) and think about what you find helpful.

★ Write a condolence letter to yourself:

    1. Express the feelings and symptoms you have,

    2. Talk about what you will miss about your lost loved one

    3. Offer to help provide to yourself what you need now.

Counseling Interventions:

★ Present the framework of Transformative Bereavement and the Grief Spiral metaphor.

★ Track changes in the story and in the way it is related.

★ Self-disclose your own losses (briefly).

★ Instill hope

★ Ask the griever to share photos of her loved one and family, and to talk in detail about each one.

★ Ask the griever if you can touch and hug her. This is grounding. You might also offer a stuffed animal to cuddle.

★ Keep a box of tissues within reach, but never offer a tissue (it can be interpreted as a signal that you want the client to stop crying).

★ Say the name of the griever's loved one as often as possible.

★ Don't be afraid to use humor. It can help to normalize and put things into perspective.

Chapter 3
Anger

When the initial shock begins to dissipate, and we are faced with the reality of the death, we often feel intense pain and anger. The pain is usually felt physically and manifests in breathing, eating, and sleeping problems; headaches, heart palpitations, tightness in the throat and/or abdominal area (grievers will often say, "I feel like I've been kicked in the stomach"); exhaustion; irritability and impatience; accidents and illness. Physical self-care such as regular exercise and vitamins, and medical and dental checkups are essential at this step.

What is anger? Anger is the expression of a sense of powerlessness and need. We feel unable to create our own energy, so we try to get it from others. And if the other person does not respond, the angry one gets even angrier – feeling even more powerless. Anger uses energy in an attempt to get energy, but if none is forthcoming there is a bigger deficit. So the angry person keeps looking for a source. You hate your boss so you kick the dog. It works, but in negative ways because that energy is never yours. It does not ultimately fulfill the need. Only you can create the energy you need. Real power is generated within yourself by what you do and feel and think and dream and dare. We are generators. We are the creators of our physical energies. We take in and transform the energy to our use. So why not the same with spiritual energy? How many grievers does it take to change a light bulb? You. Others can do it for you, but you cannot learn or recover from your grief that way and, in fact, it will only make you feel even more powerless in the long run.

Partially because of our anger, many of us feel overwhelming anxiety, and the future appears to contain nothing but a deep, dark, and empty abyss. Stated in terms of energy, even a small change releases energy that is no longer being directed, used, or focused in the old way. The amount of energy released by a death can feel like an uncontrollable tidal wave.

George was unable to sleep through the night, always waking at around 4:00 am. He had always been the son, and was anxious about his ability to take care of himself. "I was a boy. Now I'm a man," he would say.

Martha said, "I feel like there's a hole nothing will ever fill; nothing will ever be the same." She was unable to focus her energy and was sick for months during the winter following her daughter's death.

"I'm so damn angry!" Anna cried. "I don't want to be around most people because I know I'm not good company. I feel like screaming, crying, breaking things, lashing out at everyone and everything! I feel very destructive, both objects and even myself somewhat! That last part is something that has started to scare me a bit. I've never been one to give much thought of harming myself, but there have been several times in the past couple of weeks that it has become almost a consuming wish for my life to end. I really don't think I could ever actually do it, it's just that I think I wouldn't mind too much if I did die as I would not have to feel this way anymore. It just hurts so bad!"

Anxiety is a symptom of grief. When we are afraid that we cannot handle the experience of feeling the full intensity of the fear, anger and guilt arising from our grief all at once (which none of us can do) we build a protective wall, or dam, between us and what we sense as the threat of psychological annihilation resulting in the inability to function. So we keep our feelings at a distance, and we spend an enormous amount of energy keeping them at bay, and that is what feels like anxiety. In other words, anxiety is what we feel when we attempt to keep potentially overwhelming feelings of fear, anger, and guilt under control. On some level we know those feelings are there, and we also know we cannot really control them unless we confront them, but we fear that confronting them would destroy us, so we feel anxious and may even have panic attacks. But when we have adequate support, we can confront those feelings a little at a time until they seem less threatening and more manageable. Then we can let go, the dam can be allowed to crumble, the water rushes over it, and it levels out. When that happens, all the energy we had been expending to keep the dam in place becomes available to us to utilize constructively in our grief process.

It is common, and normal, for grievers at this step to experience a frightening sense of losing their sanity. A question I hear often from grievers is, "Am I crazy?" Since our society offers few models – and even less support – for healthy grieving, most of us require reassurance that the assault of emotions, thoughts, and physical symptoms we are experiencing is "normal." When given that reassurance, we are always relieved and more capable of dealing with our grief process. I have seen several clients who needed no more than that reassurance in order to move forward.

"Am I crazy?" Elizabeth, 24, asked. "It has been nearly 3 months since my grandma passed away. She died of lung cancer, and the last week of her life was

spent in the ICU at the hospital. I was there when she took her last breath. I have always been my grandma's girl. She taught me so many things about life, about manners, about my identity. I have talked about it so much, but the pain is not getting any less. My work has suffered and I was finally told last week to 'get over it' by my boss.

"My grief over losing my grandma has caused me to cling so tightly to my mom. We've always been close, but I feel like if I am not with her 24/7 that I am going to lose my mom, too. I have my own apartment and my own life. However, for the last 2 weeks I have been unable to go home, go to work, go out away from my mom. I am so afraid that I will lose her like I lost my grandma. I feel crazy, because my mom is not ill. I love my job, but I can't be there right now. I am unable to function. I do not want to 'get over' the loss of my grandma, but I need to in order to get on with my life. Is this normal? Does this get any better? Do these things go together?"

"Why me?" is another question we often ask at this step, as we begin to look externally at our changed world and notice all the people who are *not* experiencing our loss. We often feel singled out, different, victimized, even cursed or punished. We might feel that a terrible cosmic mistake has been made. "It's not fair!" we claim. Frequently our anger is directed at anyone who has not experienced the same type of loss, and thus is a reminder of what and who is no longer physically available to us.

For many years, Amy could not look at a pregnant woman or an infant without feeling rage and hatred rise within her. She deliberately avoided looking at babies. Every time Amy saw an infant, she would scream internally, "Why is he alive and James is dead? What right does that child have to be walking around in the world when mine is dead?"

Asha's son, age 12, had died accidentally 2 months earlier. She said, "I wonder if I will ever feel normal again. I just feel that I don't belong here anymore. O God, life is so unfair to give me such a beautiful boy just to take him away again. I also feel that I am constantly being judged. Am I being punished?"

Typically, our anger is also directed toward anyone who we perceive as being responsible for our loss; those who, we imagine, could have or should have done something to prevent the loss from occurring – doctors, family members, friends, witnesses in the case of a murder, etc., or transportation officials in the case of a plane, train, or bus accident. Anger might be provoked by insensitive media coverage, or by the seeming betrayal of a

God who promised rewards for being good.

Emily, 52, whose 28-year-old daughter was killed by a drunk driver, said, "I just want this life to be over. I am so tired of trying figure out how to live again. For today I have nothing to give and yet of course the world continues on. I am angry that I am here and suffering in a way that no one should ever have to suffer. I truly believe if I were God I could have come up with a better plan!"

Maria was 68 when her husband died from cancer in the hospice program. She came to the support group full of anger. When Maria's husband died, the hospice nurse – who had recently lost her own father at about the same age – was emotionally distraught and unable to stay with the widow. So she left Maria alone with her husband's body, and she had to make arrangements with the hospital to pick it up all by herself. Her anger was directed at hospice, and she spent her time in group blaming everyone who had been involved in her husband's care – which, by her own account, had been flawless up until the moment of his death.

It is important to remember that most people in our culture learn at an early age to focus on others rather than on themselves. Not only is it easier to do, but it is considered more acceptable or noble or polite. We spend so much of our time and energy talking and making judgments about what others do and choose that we would not, that we actually live much of our lives in reaction to those around us rather than in action that flows from our own core needs, values, and strengths. I mention this here because at no time are we needier than when we are grieving, and the intense need we feel for support exacerbates this problem. Feeling victimized by life, we often express anger at those around us who say things we perceive as being stupid or thoughtless or insensitive; and we tend to spend so much energy focusing on others' shortcomings and failures to care for us that we neglect self-care – which makes it harder to move forward. Focusing on others may provide a temporary distraction from feeling our own pain and confusion, but in the long run it drains our energy and prolongs the healing process. We also run the risk of alienating the very people we need for support.

Hannah said, *"People want us to forget our children, move on. I will move on and do what I can at my own pace. Darn if I will forget my son. I am tired of the stupid things people say. 'He is in a better place.' He is not in a better place, he is dead, and he should be with his family here and now. I wouldn't want him in heaven. Why would God take my child from me, that would be cruel. But yet people tell me that. How could I believe in God or anything good if I believed he took my child from me for any reason. I feel such rage and frustration, too, sometimes, and it hurts so bad. How can I feel joy again when all I feel is this terrible loss? People's lack of compassion and empathy are so sickening, too. Even within families there is no insight or understanding."*

Grievers also often feel intensely angry with their loved one for leaving them in pain, their world shattered. This can be difficult to admit, but the feeling that the loved one has broken a promise to always be there is frequently part of the response to loss. Plans had been made, dreams for the future discussed; and now it is as though the loved one has reneged without so much as an apology. "How could you do this to me?" is a question we often find ourselves screaming into the emptiness left behind.

Amy reported that on the way home from one of our sessions she expressed anger at her baby for the first time. "I found myself hitting the car seat and screaming, 'I hate you! I hate you!' over and over again."

Looking at this phase from the perspective of energy, I

believe that the feeling of anger is less about "Why me?" than about "Why now?" Confronted with a loss we cannot control, we feel powerless. This was not part of our plan; this was not what we had been working toward or expecting. Our loved one was right here – vibrant and breathing and full of life – and now she is gone! It makes no sense. It's crazy. We feel betrayed by life. We blame others in order to feel powerful and certain in the face of chaos. Some may focus on revenge – "an eye for an eye" – in an attempt to externally correct the balance of a world that seems off center. Some are willing to accept others' help, but only when it is on their terms.

Our response to our own anger is critical. In general, women seem to perceive anger as less acceptable than men do, and are more likely to deny or avoid naming it as what they are feeling. They are more likely to say, "I feel annoyed" or "It's irritating" than "I'm angry." They are more likely to get stuck in this phase because of their reluctance to confront the anger within themselves. Men have less trouble naming their anger, and they are more likely to get stuck in it because of the temporary sense of control and power it gives them.

Sophie was feeling extremely irritable, short-tempered, and tired. She would express those feelings and then immediately say, "I'm bad. I'm sorry." She knew that

*her energy was being depleted by focusing on others'
needs, but was terrified of changing her behavior and
being perceived as "selfish" by her family. She was
babysitting her grandchildren and felt guilty about
yelling at them but could not say "no" to her daughter.
She seemed to feel responsible for everyone else, but at
the same time complained that "everyone's pulling at me."*

Focusing on our own responses is helpful throughout
the grief process, but it is essential at this phase. Many of
us find that making our loved one alive in the world
through memorials, connecting with others that knew him
and sharing stories and memories, continuing projects or
activities in which he had been involved, etc., can help to
heal our anger because it shifts our focus from death to
life.

Questioning or judging our own responses and
impulses is counterproductive (e.g. "Did I say the wrong
thing?" "Why did I do that," "If I do what my impulses tell
me to do will I regret it later?" "I should have/should not
have ..."). That type of ruminating wastes energy and can
make us feel more powerless and needy. It also distracts us
from dealing with our issues. We focus on our responses
rather than on the issues themselves, and sometimes that's
why we do it. The key to healing is acceptance (e.g. "I did

that," "I want to do this," "This is what happened.").

Finally, it is at this point in the process that many of us become aware that we can feel a number of feelings at the same time – love and hate, grief and relief, anger and anguish, sadness and joy. Mixed feelings are part of every stage of the grief process, and those who grieve can become quite intimate with ambivalence.

Griever's Toolbox:

★ Exercise, take vitamins, and get medical and dental checkups.

★ Vent

★ Practice relaxation exercises.

★ Be aware of the tendency to blame others (including God) for the loss.

★ Focus on yourself, not on others.

★ Express anger in safe ways (see Appendix A).

★ Learn about cultural attitudes toward grief (see Epilogue).

★ Keep your focus on the loved one's life more than the circumstances of the death. Write a brief biography of the loved one.

★ Watch movies for distraction, learning, and fun (see Appendix A).

★ Express the value of your loved one's life through memorials (see Appendix A).

★ Connect with others that knew your loved one, and share stories and memories.

★ Find at least one friend who has also experienced a loss, and to talk to that person as often as possible.

★ Continue projects or activities in which the loved one had been involved.

★ Draw pictures that express your feelings.

★ When you get angry at others who say or do the

"wrong" things, tell them what you need and what is not helpful.

★ Write a condolence letter to yourself, expressing the feelings and symptoms you have had, what you will miss about the lost loved one, and an offer to help provide what you need now.

Counseling Interventions:

★ Closely monitor the griever's physical health.
★ Normalize the griever's experiences and reassure him about his sanity.
★ Acknowledge and normalize anger directed toward others, but always bring the focus back to the griever.
★ Ask whether the griever is angry with the one who died. If you do not ask, the griever may not tell you.

Chapter 4
Bargaining

It is not only our feelings that are ambivalent, but also our perception of the finality of the loss. In the bargaining phase, because we often feel we are being punished and that the loss was some sort of cosmic error, we frantically search for a way to reverse it.

Ida's daughter died at the age of 11 in an auto accident. She said, "So many times in the past 9 months I've begged God to let me do it over. I know how to change that day. One little question and my Amanda would be here with us. I can do it right next time! Just give me one more chance, please! My pleading seems to fall on deaf ears because time continues to move away from that day."

The search often feels like a continual cycle of reaching out and running into walls. We try to maintain our old behavior patterns in the face of a fundamental alteration of our landscape; we try to live out our roles and participate in activities as we did before the loss happened, as if the road ahead had not been rerouted with what appear to be detours, and we run headlong into barriers. We are confronted with constant, inescapable reminders that what *was* is no more. This is part of the separation anxiety that grievers usually feel – similar to the separation anxiety of a 2-year-old who is discovering her own autonomy for the first time.

Since Jessica's death, Martha had been unable to go into a shopping mall. Every store reminded her of how much fun they used to have together window-shopping and enjoying each other's company. One day, with the support of a good friend, Martha decided to challenge herself and go into a department store. She did well until they got to the clothing department. All of a sudden, Martha felt Jessica's presence and saw her in all the clothes she would have wanted to buy. Martha panicked and said, "I just wanted to run and scream. . .just scream and never stop. I cried all the way home. It was like she was right there beside me. I just cannot do it!"

We make promises to God, the universe, or our loved ones to do better or to be a better partner/parent/friend/child if only our loss can be made not to have happened. These promises or resolutions may not even be conscious, but are evident in a sense of expectation – a feeling of waiting for the world to set itself right once again – and some type of preparation for that event. As it becomes evident that this expectation will not be fulfilled, we teach ourselves that our world has, indeed, been irreversibly changed.

Samantha was 55 when her husband died suddenly. She awoke one morning to find him dead in the bed beside her. Samantha expressed the conviction that Ryan would come back if she did the "right" things. She talked a lot about how she would make improvements in her life, take better care of herself, and do what Ryan had always wanted her to do. She had a dream in which Ryan told her he would be coming back.

At this point, we may also try to postpone the necessity of dealing with the reality of the loss. "Just let me see/touch/hear/hug my loved one once more, and then I'll accept it," we plead. One positive and potentially healing consequence of this desire to feel our loved one close once again is that it sends many of us on a spiritual search. We begin to investigate such concepts as life after death, spirit communication, meditation, religious writings, and other paths toward understanding. Grievers often see and feel the physical touch or hug of their loved ones in dreams, and many grievers report feeling, smelling, hearing, and/or seeing their presence while awake. Hope can be instilled by these experiences, as grievers learn that their loved one – while no longer physically accessible to them – still exists in some way. Here again, the widening of focus facilitates growth and forward movement. Spiritual or psychological experiences of this type should never be characterized as "hallucinations," unless the griever has already been clinically diagnosed with a severe personality disorder.

Jessica's birthday was just before Christmas, and Martha said, "We cried our eyes out." That night she had a dream about Jessica, who said, "Mama, I just don't know why you worry about me so much. I'm so happy!" Martha said Jessica felt very physical in the dream, and she knew it was a real visitation. She knew Jessica was still with her spiritually. She told me about a star that she saw every morning on the way to work, and talked to as though it were Jessica. She had ongoing conversations with Jessica throughout the day, and sometimes heard a response. I encouraged her to accept those experiences as real, and to accept that Jessica's physical death did not mean the end of their relationship – simply the beginning of a different kind of relationship; one in which Martha would have to continue alone those aspects of it that were physical.

Ida said, "I find it comforting to imagine Amanda and I planned this life, even though it is unbearably hard right now. I'm searching for an answer to why she had to die so young. An active, kind-hearted girl that was loved and respected by many. Why her, when there are so many mean, hateful ones still enjoying their lives? In my search I've read many types of books and listened to many speakers. I've taken bits and pieces from each that give me comfort. I love to discuss beliefs with anyone. . . I'm still searching."

Because our focus is on trying to reverse the loss and bring our loved one back, it is important to keep in mind that our loved one will always be a part of us and that we were a part of the relationship, too. That might sound obvious and simplistic, but many of us focus so intensely on our loss that we forget that and think of the relationship with our loved one as being incorporated in their physical presence.

Another facet of this step is guilt. Having failed in the attempt to make someone else responsible for our loss, we try taking responsibility ourselves. This can result in an agonizing, sometimes even debilitating, sense of guilt. The process is not linear, so we can also find ourselves going from trying to take responsibility to blaming others, and back again.

What is guilt? In many people, guilt becomes the familiar feeling accepted in exchange for fear – which, no matter how often, can never feel familiar. Now, what is the origin of fear? A sense of not being in control, things happening to one. And what is the source of guilt? A sense that one had complete control of the situation. Two ends of the same pole. Rather than face the fear of being unable to control our lives, we say to ourselves, "If only I had done _____ this would not have happened," or "I should have/would have/could have _____." We try to give ourselves the illusion of control because it is too scary to feel out of control. Since ambiguity is so hard to deal with any time, and especially so in stress, we flee from the fear possibilities to the guilt certainties, rather than live out of control and uncertain. The path back from guilt is the path through our fears. We cannot move out of guilt without dealing with those fears.

Martha cried as she told me the story of Jessica's surgery and subsequent death again – this time in more detail. She said, "I wouldn't let her go." I reminded her that she did let her go in the end and asked if she felt guilty about that. "No, not about that," she sobbed, "but she was my baby and I should have known what was wrong with her. I should have been able to make her go to the doctor sooner."

George said that what he felt most guilty about was not being in the hospital room with his mom when she died. He saw her lying there, hooked up to machines, "in bad shape," and could not stay. After calling his mother's sister, his favorite aunt, he went outside for a smoke while waiting for her to arrive. It was then that his mom died.

Mark's dad had died when he was 28 – 20 years before he came to see me. Like his dad, he was an alcoholic. He had been in recovery for 4 years and was just beginning to feel again after having frozen himself since the age of 16. Mark's dad died in a nursing home 2 months after their last telephone conversation. During that conversation, Mark became angry and hung up on him. "I felt terribly guilty about that and it sent me into a tailspin," he said at our first session. "We never said goodbye."

I believe that there is a normal level of guilt associated with a loved one's death that persists even after we have dealt with it. We feel – as unreasonable as we may know it to be – that there was something we might have done to change or ameliorate the outcome. Parents feel especially responsible, as their job is to nurture and protect their children. Whether guilt keeps us stuck in the grief process is really the only way we have of differentiating normal from resistant guilt.

Emma said, "I have many regrets. I can never say 'sorry' to Matt for yelling at him to get into bed when all he wanted to do was give me a hug. I can never say 'sorry' to Matt for not giving him a kiss or cuddle goodbye the day he died because I was so angry with him. Sure, maybe Matt has forgiven me my mistakes but I will never forgive myself. I can never change them. . . and I hate that! I have such a long way to go before I can look at myself in the mirror. And I knew that Matt was going to die. For many years I would wake up out of my sleep not being able to breathe and crying because I had just dreamed that Matt had died and I could see his father and I at his funeral. The strange thing is that I forgot about these dreams until about 3 months after Matt died. I then remembered, and ever since then I have felt guilty for not taking heed of the warnings. Guilt is the worst emotion that I am having. I just don't know what to do with it. Guilt is what is destroying me."

Sometimes guilt is a result of cultural influences. For example, someone who would have an abortion and never look back, might feel guilty if she knows that those around her believe that having an abortion is morally wrong under any circumstances.

Some grievers may resist confronting their guilt because it feels like their final, fragile connection to their loved one. They may fear that letting go of their guilt means letting go of the last link they have to the physical relationship and being left with nothing at all.

From the moment Amy realized she was pregnant, she had no control. She was only 18 and she and her husband were living with his family. She already had a beautiful son, and did not want another child. "I hated it!" she said. "I refused to take care of myself. But when I didn't miscarry I decided it must be meant to be and got excited about it again." She became ill and was forced by the family to go to the hospital for a Caesarean section while her son had a 104-degree fever and she wanted to stay home and take care of him. At the hospital, her blood pressure dropped dangerously. She was given medication that caused her baby to have a heart attack, and when she tried to reach out to help him she was given oxygen that made her pass out. Afterwards, "they made all the arrangements. They put all the baby furniture away before I got home. I had no say in what happened at the funeral. They made James look like a slut with all that makeup. I didn't want to go to the funeral, but they made me. Then they wouldn't let me go to see him at the cemetery until Easter [a month later]. No one would talk about him. They gave me a hat and a blanket, but I don't think they're really his. I know there was nothing I could do, but my pain is all I have of him," she said, "it's the only thing that's mine. I can control that."

Reframing this from a spiritual perspective, reminding grievers that their loved ones do not want or need them to be in pain in order to feel connected to them, that their loved ones will be there for them no matter what they feel, is often helpful for those who believe in an afterlife. Another helpful image is that of the umbilical cord, which must be cut in order for both parent and child to grow and develop.

The resolution or, at least, the understanding and acceptance – of guilt is usually the key that opens the door to moving toward a changed and future relationship with the loss, with the loved one, and with life. The slightest change in perspective at this point can create an opening. For example, when one client's perception of guilt shifted from a defensive, "I could have changed it" to "Who knows, it might not have changed but it might have," that indicated that she was ready to take a tentative step forward.

When we question, second-guess, analyze, judge, or try to control our feelings, we stop feeling, short circuit the process, and focus our energy on maintaining the dam. Guilt keeps us in the past and/or focusing on what did *not* happen. When we can face our fears; when we can take responsibility for and accept all of our feelings without judgment or censorship, we are better able to face and accept the opportunities that our lives offer us as paths of learning and growth. You cannot get where you want to go facing away from your direction. And you cannot deal with what never *was*.

Sometimes grievers feel guilty when having fun. As with any guilt feeling, the question to ask is, "What's the fear?" In this case, it is usually about forgetting, the sense that if we are not thinking about our loved one every second, we will lose them a second time, and this time it will be because of our own choice to move forward.

Many people ask, "What about guilt that is justified? What if I did something to contribute to the person's death?" Again, the question is still: "What's the fear?" Is it of yourself, your potential for evil or selfish action or sin? In cases like that, we are challenged is to accept ourselves with all of our imperfections, and to do something to make amends if we feel the need to do so. Again, acceptance is the key. When we cannot accept something that is part of us, we cannot make choices about it and we cannot leave it in the past. If we judge ourselves, or feel we need to be judged, we compare ourselves to someone or something else. We focus externally instead of dealing with ourselves as we really are.

The resolution of guilt is a key to recovery from grief, but resolution does not necessarily mean total absence of guilt. It means the acceptance of whatever level might remain after dealing with it.

Griever's Toolbox:

★ Ponder the metaphor of constantly running into walls.

★ Be aware of your anticipation of the loved one coming back.

★ Explore spiritual and/or religious beliefs, meditation, prayer, inspirational books and websites, dreams and dream journaling (see Appendix A).

★ Remember that your loved one will always continue to be present as part of your identity, and that you were part of the relationship, too.

★ Think about what you would choose as a symbolic representation of your loved one (e.g., butterfly, flower, star, song, angel, airplane, etc.).

★ Write your loved one a letter or have an Empty Chair conversation expressing any regrets for what was unsaid or undone, or guilt feelings for what was said or done.

★ Do the I Wish I Had... I Wish I Hadn't writing exercise (Appendix A).

★ Ponder whether you have the power to keep someone else alive.

★ If you believe in an afterlife, understand that your loved one does not want or need you to be in pain in order to feel connected. Use the umbilical cord metaphor: The cord must be cut for both parent and child to grow and develop. If it is not cut, both die.

★ Make sure your support system is sufficient. Fill out the My Support System worksheet (Appendix A).

★ Learn (and keep in mind) the *Serenity Prayer*:
> Spirit of All,
> Grant me the serenity to accept the things I cannot change,
> The courage to change the things I can,
> And the wisdom to know the difference.

Counseling Interventions:

★ Compare the griever's anxiety to the separation anxiety of a 2-year-old.

★ Introduce, normalize, and explore the topic of guilt. Explain that guilt is a way to control fear. Allow the griever to express all the guilt she feels.

★ If the griever is resistant, reframe her guilt as the last link to the physical relationship.

★ Listen for a shift in perspective indicating the willingness to let go, and reinforce it.

Chapter 5
Depression

How many tears is it possible to cry? That is a question to which grievers often learn this answer: There is no limit. Tears often flow – seemingly randomly, uncontrollably, and with a life of their own – from the moment of loss. And, as we begin to come to terms with the reality of our loss, our anxiety decreases and a sense of profound sadness comes in its wake. The search ends, along with the expectation that our loved one will physically return and that life will return to "normal."

Emma said, "I have no energy to fight today. I am no longer Emma. I am a grieving mom. I have heavy muscles in my face that make it too hard to smile. Hell, I don't even want to smile. So my mask is neatly laid to rest beside my bed so I can put it on again tomorrow. Not that I want to wear that mask, but I'm too ugly to the average world without it. No one really wants to see what lies beneath this mask. I have to wear heavy clothing, too, or everyone will see this thud that I have constantly coming out of my chest. The one that is missing a beat. It's been raining here lately but not outside, inside. The rain is my tears and they are flooding my house – which is no longer a home. It is four walls of nothing. So I will go back to my bed, look up at the ceiling and try to figure out how I will make it through tomorrow. I'm sorry, Matt, for being weak but sometimes I just don't know how to live without you."

The dam breaks, and the overwhelming feelings of loss that have been held at bay by fear, anger, and guilt rush like a tidal wave over the crumbling wall. This is an indication of moving forward in the process – the sadness is a healthy and hopeful sign. Much energy has been directed toward maintaining that wall and the illusion of control; and, once the release occurs – although it can feel scary and overwhelming at first – the tidal wave settles down and levels out, and energy becomes available to cope with the change. Typically, we do not know how to focus the energy that becomes available after the tidal wave, and a sense of control is vital in order to prevent clinical depression.

George had not come for counseling for a month and a half. When he came in he looked exhausted and disheveled, which was unusual since his appearance had always been clean and well-groomed. He said he felt out of control of his life and was not feeling good about himself. He had been going to bed early in the morning, sleeping until the afternoon, and spending most of his time watching TV. He felt unsafe, vulnerable, helpless, and alone. He had been feeling acutely the reality of his own mortality and the fragility of physical life. I suggested he give himself something to get up for in the morning, and that he set his alarm for the same time each morning no matter what. He came back after having done that and reported feeling much better.

At this point, grievers typically describe themselves as feeling "lost" and "helpless." Nothing in our physical or emotional landscape seems familiar. Nothing we knew or were interested in before seems worthwhile. We are confused and disoriented, and incapable of either continuing our fruitless search for what was or discovering new ways of being in the world. We may become clinically depressed if we begin to focus on our feelings of helplessness and disorientation. We may so desperately yearn for an end to the pain that we consider suicide. Ordinarily, however, it is at this point in the grief process where the opportunity for growth and forward movement is greatest. We must begin to relinquish the past before we can move toward the future.

Martha told me, "It's like you had somebody by your side and now you're out in this big strange world all by yourself. I feel lost." I asked her if she ever physically got lost. She told me that once Jessica, she, and her husband were out on their boat. Jessica was driving, and when Martha looked around for a landmark she saw nothing. "I didn't even see a seagull." She panicked and felt "petrified," starting yelling at her husband to "go this way, go that way, but there is no this way or that way. You can't go back and you can't go forward. There was no calming me down. And then I got mad at both of them for getting me lost. Then we saw a barge in the distance and went toward it and found land. But I was scared to death. After we got home I went straight to the store and bought a GPS. I'm lost again. But this time I don't have Jessica laughing at me and telling me it will be alright."

After his dad died, Mark went into a deep depression that lasted for a year. He said he felt "immobilized. I quit drinking and stayed home. I didn't work, didn't go out, just stayed in my bathrobe and slippers all day. I felt helpless and I hate that feeling. I thought I was nuts."

This is another point in the process at which some grievers will be medicated, because grief depression is often misdiagnosed as clinical depression. An important study found. that, while medication is a remedy for depression, it has no differential effect on the intensity of grief. They concluded that the symptoms of depression may be more biological, and thus more treatable with psychotropic medications, while grief is the result of loss and the problems grievers encounter as they face the tasks of change. They suggested that longer or more specialized psychotherapy might be necessary to aid in the resolution of grief. And then they made a statement which, in the light of how grief and loss have been perceived by Western society – and particularly by the medical community – struck me as potentially revolutionary: "A . . . possibility, however, is that persistence of grief is not necessarily abnormal or pathological. Preoccupation with the memory of the lost [loved one] might be the normal or necessary sequela of genuine attachment and part of a necessary sustenance of life" (Reynolds, Pasternak, Frank, Perel, Cornes, Houck, Mazumdar, Dew & Kupfer, 1999).

The differences between grief and clinical depression may seem subtle to the casual observer, but they are fundamental and significant:

1. Clinical depression does not always involve a recognizable loss, while grief involves a recognizable, and usually current, loss.
2. The reactions of someone with clinical depression are

intense and persistent, while a griever's reactions are initially intense and then variable.

3. The mood of someone with clinical depression is consistently low, flat, chronic, and often expresses an absence of emotion, while the mood of a griever changes, tends to be acute rather than prolonged, and is heightened when thinking about the loss.

4. The behavior of someone with clinical depression involves the refusal of previously enjoyed activities, a lack of enthusiasm, and difficulty enjoying activity, while a griever's behavior is much more variable. It shifts from being able to share pain to wanting to be alone, and the response to enjoyable activities is variable.

5. Someone who is clinically depressed tends toward unexpressed self-directed anger, while someone who is grieving directs most anger externally.

6. The sadness of clinical depression has restricted variability. Its expression is either inhibited or uncontrolled. The sadness of grief varies, with periodic episodes of crying.

7. The clinically depressed person's thoughts are preoccupied with themselves and with self-blame, worthlessness, and hopelessness. The griever's thoughts are preoccupied with the lost loved one, confusion, and disorientation to present

circumstances.

8. Clinical depression usually involves a previous history of depression or other psychiatric disorder, while grief does not.

9. Someone who is clinically depressed has chronic insomnia or excessive sleeping, often with regular early morning awakening. Someone who is grieving has periodic difficulties or disturbances in sleep patterns.

10. The clinically depressed person's expressed imagery is self-punitive and access to dreams is limited, while the griever often has vivid dreams along with the capacity for imagery and fantasy.

11. The hopelessness and helplessness of someone with clinical depression limit their responsiveness to others, while someone who is grieving responds to warmth and reassurance.

12. The clinically depressed person's focus is on themselves. The griever's focus is on their lost loved one.

13. When in the presence of a clinically depressed person, others tend to feel irritated or want to keep their distance. When in the presence of a griever, others tend to want to reach out and feel empathy or sympathy.

It is important to keep in mind that, although there are many differences between grief and clinical depression, grief can lead to clinical depression if untreated.

We now begin to realize the nature and implications of what we have lost. There are often financial and social changes that must be addressed. Income may decrease, or increase; friendships that were dependent on the presence or role of a partner or child or parent may be shaken or ended. The full impact of the harsh reality that our loved one will not ever be physical again hits hard, along with the realization that dreams of the future that involved that person no longer exist as possibilities. We often feel we have lost what we will never have.

Mark mourned the loss of his father in relation to his own grandchildren-to-be. His father would never know his great-grandchildren. "I imagine him coming to visit," he said. "I can see it so clearly. He'd come up to our porch where Nadia and I would be sitting and waiting, rocking in our rocking chairs together. Then our children would come out of the house with their children, bringing lemonade and sandwiches, and they'd help my dad sit down. He would then 'allow' all of us to attend to him and he'd grin shyly. He would have been so happy. He was such a lonely guy."

Emma said, "There are so many new things around

now that Matt would have loved. There is a new cartoon on TV that is all about Jackie Chan. Matt loved Jackie Chan and Bruce Lee. There is a new PlayStation game that is BMX bike racing. Matt would have just bugged and bugged me to get it for him. There are new winter clothes that he would have loved. . . everywhere. And then there's all the new songs. I can't get away from music as it's everywhere. How will I ever get through this?"

Griever's Toolbox:

★ Use this metaphor: Feelings of profound loss and anxiety are like water in a river, held at bay by a dam of fear, anger, and guilt. It takes enormous energy to maintain that wall and the illusion of control. When the dam breaks, feelings rush like a tidal wave over the crumbling wall. Now energy becomes available to cope with your changed world. Although it feels scary and overwhelming at first, the tidal wave settles down and levels out. Water always seeks its own level.

★ Set an alarm clock or timer for a specific amount of time, cry and /or express whatever you need to express within that safe, time-limited space, then stop when the time is up and give yourself a small reward.

★ The Grief Release exercise (Appendix A) can be helpful at this point as a way to focus and aid in letting go.

★ Give yourself something to look forward to each day.

★ Explore the feelings of being lost, helpless, and disoriented. Think about previous similar feelings and experiences of getting lost, and how you dealt with them.

★ Draw pictures of what life was like before and after the loss.

★ Explore Secondary Losses (e.g., lost roles, activities, relationships, expectations, etc.) (Appendix A).

★ Differentiate between what really has been lost, and

what will never be in the future.

★ Continue to monitor your physical health and engage in physical exercise.

★ Understand that intense emotional pain is a temporary outcome of loss, and necessary for dealing with change and growth.

Counseling Interventions:

★ Emphasize structure, schedule, and control.

★ Reframe this phase as a positive indication of forward movement and an opportunity for growth – a beginning of letting go.

★ Listen for suicidal ideation (and take appropriate legal steps if necessary).

★ Address changes in the griever's finances and/or social status.

★ Do not recommend psychotropic medication, unless you are sure of a diagnosis of clinical depression or the client is totally unable to function.

Chapter 6
Acceptance

Arrival at acceptance of the loss is only possible when the thoughts and feelings of all the previous steps or phases have been accepted and worked through. We often feel an inner peace we had never before experienced, and are surprised that this peacefulness arose in the wake of the chaos created by our loss. Initially we distrust the feeling, and may even find it scary because it is new and unfamiliar. The pain is still present, and often extremely intense, but it is present less frequently. Moments of peace begin to elongate into hours and then days, and when the pain comes it is greeted like a familiar companion and is less disorienting than it was at the beginning of the Loss stage (spiral of emotions). There are moments of intense joy – although they may still be followed by guilt over feeling such joy, as it means having chosen to loosen the bonds that kept the loved one present – and more of a balance between laughter and tears.

Five months after his mom's death, George told me he was thinking more clearly, was a lot more calm and more focused. "Before I wasn't thinking about the next step, but now I'm more aware of what is ahead." He was planning on selling his parents' house and seeing it as "a new start." He said, "Before it was all a bad dream and I kept thinking it will go away. Now it's real." He added, "People who haven't been through this don't understand it. Nothing compares to it."

At this point in the process, we have stopped struggling to avoid the reality of what has occurred. Many grievers feel they have acquired a new and deeper wisdom about death, and a more sensitive appreciation of life. Priorities have changed. We are less materialistic, more spiritual, more empathetic to the pain of others, more patient and accepting, less driven and judgmental. "Life is not what I thought it was," many grievers exclaim. We learn that it is less about the acquisition of material comforts and more about an ongoing process of growth, learning, and sharing with fellow travelers on the path. We open our hearts and arms more easily to others in pain, no longer able to turn away and pretend it will never happen to us. We also often acquire a new appreciation for our own inner resources and strength. Many will say things like, "I never knew I could survive something like this," or "I thought that if he died, I would die, too."

As the first anniversary of her daughter's death

approached, Martha said she was feeling stronger, like she could handle anything. Her priorities had changed, and taking time to be with people seemed more important than work or making money. "I think straighter than I did, but my heart still hurts," she said. "It's hard and it hurts, but I'm starting to accept the fact that she's gone home. But I know she'll be waiting for me." Martha remarked that her strength surprised her. When it first happened, all she wanted was to be with Jessica.

During the first year of grief, much energy is focused on anticipating and dealing with "firsts": the first birthday of our loved one without their physical presence, our first birthday without that presence, the first holiday season, the first spring – which is often very painful as we perceive that the world is coming to life again but our loved one is not – the first New Year's Eve that ushers in the first calendar year that will not contain our loved one's physical presence, and the first time many activities that had meaning in our relationship are faced alone. We often learn that the anticipation of these events is more painful than the reality when it occurs. By the time of the first anniversary, it is common to hear grievers report a sense of closure, a feeling that they have come "full circle" and have successfully navigated the calendar on their own. The next cycle seems less threatening and more familiar.

So, why isn't this the end of the grief process? Many of us who expect that Acceptance will be the end of our journey are surprised and disappointed when we reach this point and then sense ourselves returning to revisit the process from what often feels like the beginning. For, while we have accepted the loss of our loved one, we have yet to accept our own changed identity. We don't know who we are anymore, and the question I usually hear at this point is "Now what?"

Griever's Toolbox:

★ Be aware of the possibility that you might experience guilt about feeling peace or joy.

★ Focus on your strengths.

★ Explore what you have learned about life and priorities.

★ Reach out to others in pain.

★ Since this phase usually coincides with the first anniversary of the death, plan a commemorative ceremony or ritual.

★ Engage in fun, energizing rewards for the hard work accomplished so far.

★ Learn about the next stage of the grief process.

Counseling Interventions:

★ Praise the griever for having stopped struggling to avoid the reality of what happened and for letting go.

Stage 2: Return

What we call the beginning is often an ending
And to make an end is to make a beginning.
The end is where we start from.

– T.S. Eliot (from Four Quartets)

Chapter 7
Return

Thinking again about the image of the spiral of change, the Loss stage is represented by the line that moves forward and the Return by the line that curves backward into a loop. This is a stage that often feels like regression. In reality, when we are committed to the grief process, it is a continuation of forward motion, but in a different direction or dimension.

Another type of perceived regression that should not be confused with the Return stage can occur when we experience any subsequent loss. The effect of multiple losses is cumulative. Each loss will bring us emotionally back to the Loss stage, and may make our response seem like an overreaction. Or, when one loss is almost immediately followed by another loss, there will be an under-reaction because we are incapable of dealing with more. In both cases the level of intensity of the response may seem abnormal, but in fact it is a normal reaction when we are forced to refocus in the face of the chaotic feelings and/or circumstances of a traumatic experience.

Eight years after her baby James's death, Amy

witnessed the stillbirth of her brother's daughter. She was in the hospital room when Zoe was born dead, and even though they were informed in advance that Zoe would be stillborn, Amy "flipped out." "I asked if I could hold her," she said with a lump in her throat, *"but the next thing I remember was running down the hallway hitting walls and I couldn't breathe. But I went back. I felt I had a second chance to say goodbye to my son. I apologized to both of them and begged God to breathe my breath into Zoe – to bring one back. Then when my Karin was born, I felt like I was going crazy. I looked at her and saw James. I was terrified something would happen to her, and before she was born I didn't choose a name or buy anything – no baby clothes, furniture, not even diapers – just in case she died. When my due date came I said, 'I'm not going to the hospital. As long as she's in my belly she's alive.' "*

To continue our discussion of the Return stage, while the end of the fundamental momentum of the Loss stage brings a deeper sense of peace and acceptance and wisdom, it also brings a deeper awareness of loss. There is usually a sense of greater separation from deceased loved ones in terms of time, distance, and our own psychological development. This can be extremely painful as we begin to realize that our lives are continuing while those of our loved ones seem frozen in time, space, and memory. At this point there are many physical events in our lives that our loved ones have not shared; many thoughts, feelings, and learnings that our loved ones seemingly have had no relationship to; many memories created that do not contain the physical presence of our loved ones. The chasm that separates the living and dead seems to widen, and life seems to move ahead inexorably and uncontrollably.

We have accepted our new reality that does not contain the physical presence of our loved one, but we have yet to accept the ways in which we are different in it.

So, we return to where we were before the loss, and have to deal with the fact that we are not there anymore. It's like going back to a childhood home and everything looks smaller or different. Not only has it changed and aged, but our perceptions have changed and grown, and if we do not accept the change in our perceptions, we cannot go back there as we are, only as we were. It is a similar experience to being at a holiday dinner where everyone in the family automatically falls into old familiar roles, and we leave there thinking, "That wasn't who I am now."

There is a disconnect between who we think we are and who we have become. It is not just our loved one who has left, but our selves as we knew them. We grieve ourselves. If we do not go back and discover how we, too, have moved on, we will fall back into those old roles. We will be forever haunted by "back then" and "once upon a time" as if *then* were *now* – and it is not.

Chapter 8
Denial

Our identity has changed with the loss of our loved one. Many secondary losses also become evident at this time. All the roles that we have played in relation to the one who has been lost are also gone. We are no longer the child, parent, partner, spouse, grandchild, sibling, or friend. "Who am I?" is the question grievers usually ask at this point. We often feel out of control, fearful, and confused. We do not recognize who we are and we do not know who to be. It sometimes feels as if we are experiencing a second adolescence, with all of its doubts and discomforts, and like adolescence, this is a time for identity re-formation. When our grief process first takes us into the Return phase, we cannot be who we were and we cannot see who we will be in the future; so in an effort to protect the identity of our selves as we knew them, we deny the change and try to make our changed selves function in the same old patterns and routines.

"One night last week I had a dream about Megan that has really pulled me under," said Emily, who had lost her daughter 14 months earlier. "I dreamed that she came

back, that God thought we deserved a second chance. It was so wonderful to see her again, to have her home with us. She came back very very sick, but I knew that I could make her well again and I was just so grateful for this second chance. If it is possible, my heart broke even more when I woke up and I realized there will never be any second chances for us – not in this life anyway. I have been struggling so much ever since. I feel so exhausted. I am so tired of trying to go on without her. Nothing feels right without her here on this earth. Nothing. I am just so very tired."

Having a new sense of our own strength but no clear direction, all directions look the same – no single way of life or self-expression seems more compelling or personally meaningful than any other. One of the hallmarks of this phase is that making decisions is often anxiety provoking.

Faced with a decision of whether to end an unfulfilling relationship, Chloe was ambivalent. On one hand she said, "I feel differently about him. I've pulled back. I'm tired of it." On the other hand, she said, "I'll be by myself again. I don't want to be alone. When I'm alone I spend too much money and gain weight . . . trying to fill the void with food, material things, going immediately into another relationship. Two years ago I didn't think I could make it alone. Now I do but I don't want to. I can feel the change inside. It's pretty weird. Maybe we could deal with my repressed feelings and fears one at a time?"

Emily said, "Making decisions is something that is driving me crazy. Every single decision I make seems to take on huge proportions. And no matter which way I decide, it always feels wrong! I am so tired of this. What does this mean and how do I change it? I was planning to go to a grief conference, but it just didn't seem to be falling into place financially, etc. So yesterday I finally let it go. This morning I am thinking, Well maybe it is still not too late . . .aaarrrggghhh. Why can't I just accept what is. Why am I torturing myself in this way?"

At the same time, just as we may have been surprised at our own ability to cope immediately following our loss, we are often filled with a sense of self-satisfaction at having come this far in the process. Although we do not yet quite trust it, and express doubts about how permanent our new feelings of calm and peace may be, we look back in wonder and say things like, "I never thought I could come this far after what happened to me. I'm stronger than I thought I was." As in the Loss stage, we tell our story over and over again, but this time the emphasis is on how we managed to survive and overcome the obstacles on our journey.

Emily said, "I used to be much more outgoing, now I am quieter (easier?) to be around. I listen more and I appreciate even more the little things in life and the people especially who are truly present for me. In many ways I have changed for the better. Not that I was bad to begin with! But o I have gone through the fire, been reduced to ashes, and the new me that will rise . . . is rising. . . will be stronger and more beautiful than ever! Because I now have an angel that is with me guiding me, leading me, loving me every step of the way. And I now know what real living is about!"

Since it is so much easier at this point for us to focus on past accomplishments than it is to deal with our changed identities, there is a danger of getting stuck and being unable to move into new ways of being. Complicating this tendency is the disappointment we often feel when we seem to be going backwards in the process. Grief can be exhausting, and we may feel like giving up. Under stress, we naturally fall back into familiar behavior patterns – no matter how painful they may be – because the known is always easier to deal with than the unknown. Remaining in the past with our now-familiar companion, pain, can seem seductive. Or we may try to deny the pain, and learn how to avoid anything painful or anxiety-provoking – focusing on keeping busy, materialism, and problem solving. But widening, rather than narrowing, our perspective, and finding new things that are meaningful and fulfilling is the key to healing.

Chloe had been tempted to fall back into the caretaking role in her relationship, but said, "I'm concerned about him but not going to drop everything just to do what he needs. The urge was there, but I stopped and thought about it this time. I see that I've repeated the same patterns over and over. Now I hope and feel I won't do that anymore. I feel different."

Anxiety often recurs in this phase. The anxiety of the Loss stage is a symptom of the attempt to keep from being overwhelmed by intense feelings of fear, anger, and guilt. Associated with that is the tension between trying to keep our loved one in the present, while knowing she or he is physically in the past. Anxiety in the Return stage is a symptom of the tension between trying to stay as we were in the past, and being – at least, partially – in the future. Again, it's similar to identity formation in adolescence.

At this step we may talk incessantly about the past. We often seem to confuse the present with the past, and we talk about ourselves and our emotional responses as though they were the same as before, while intellectually acknowledging that our feelings, values, and perceptions have changed. It is helpful at this point – but not always possible – to be able to sort out which feelings, roles, values, and perceptions belong to the past; which to the present; and which to the future.

Amy talked about being unable to take time off from work when she was sick. She insisted that going to work every day was not a choice, but a necessity – even though her husband also worked and made enough money to take care of their family. She focused on scarcity and identified with loss, feeling there was never enough. During one session she cried as she reported having blurted out at the dinner table, "I don't eat because I make sure there's enough for my daughter!" She seemed to have frozen her image of herself in time and could not see how she or her life had changed. She was proud of being a "survivor," but it was a static vision.

While in the Loss phase of Denial it is helpful for us to focus on concrete actions that externalize our loss (e.g., journaling) in order to be able to look back and chart our own progress, in this phase it is helpful to focus on concrete actions that externalize the identity of the loved one in order to be able to better focus on the recreation of our own identities. So memorial activities that involve ceremony, remembrance, and the creation of a concrete place or object or internet website that symbolizes our loved one and represents the continuation of her spirit in the physical world are small but extremely healing steps that can free some of our energies from their stranglehold focus on that part of our loved one that is no longer present in the physical world.

Amy missed going to James's gravesite. She had not been there in over a year because it was so far away. She mentioned that she had been thinking about "adopting" a baby in a nearby cemetery. "There's so many of them that don't get flowers. It looks like nobody's visiting them, and I thought I could take care of one of them."

Griever's Toolbox:

★ Use this metaphor: The grief process is a spiral. Sometimes it takes a backwards movement to go forward, but one never goes back to the exact same place as before. You have changed and learned through this grief process, so you go back in a different way.

★ Be aware of your sense of distance from your loved one and grief over roles that have been lost.

★ Understand your anxiety over making decisions. How can you decide what to do when you don't know who you are.

★ Continue to focus on your strengths and on what you have learned so far. Do the My Strengths and My Strengths Adjectives exercises (Appendix A).

★ Notice that when you re-tell "the story," there is more of a focus on positives.

★ You may distrust of your new feelings of peace and calm. Be aware of the possibility of exhaustion - a tendency to want to give up or avoid more pain.

★ Begin sorting out which feelings, roles, values, and perceptions belong to the past; which to the present; and which to the future.

★ Engage in activities that externalize the identity of your loved one so that you can focus on your own identity (e.g., memorial activities that involve ceremony, remembrance, and the creation of a concrete place, object, plaque, or website) (see Appendix A).

★ Make some changes in your home. This helps alleviate the feeling that the only thing that has changed is the absence of the loved one.

★ Try new things.

Counseling Interventions:

★ Explore and normalize the griever's feelings of regression.

★ Discuss the Return stage as identity formation (or re-formation).

★ Listen for tense confusion – the griever's self-perception of being the same emotionally while intellectually acknowledging that he has changed.

Chapter 9
Anger

Anger, guilt, and depression are more complex in the Return stage than in the Loss stage for several reasons: 1. There is a sense of going backwards (even though we cannot go back to the exact same place we were, because we have changed), 2. Even as we sense ourselves going backwards to the beginning of the grief process, at the same time we feel farther away from our loved one in terms of both time and our own development, and 3. We know we have changed and we can see many of those changes as positive, but we do not yet have a clear idea of who we are.

When we can no longer deny the reality of our changed identity, we often revisit feelings of intense pain and anger. The distinguishing characteristic of anger at this stage is that it is directed more at our own lost identity than at attempts to place external blame and assign responsibility for our situation. We often make such poignant declarations as "I will never be a grandmother" or "I have always thought of myself as his wife. I feel like no one now!" Feeling powerless to change our new reality back into the one it was supposed to be, or should have been, we recite endlessly our litany of what will never be. We focus on what is not, and never will be, in our future because we cannot yet imagine the future as it will be. Of course, focusing on what is not and will never be real, makes us feel even more powerless. It is too difficult at this point in the process to understand that the future is beyond the scope of our present vision and to trust that it will be as fulfilling and meaningful as the past. Our anger may serve the additional purposes of keeping feelings of sadness and despair at a distance, and providing a temporary "jolt" of power.

At this point we talk a lot about what our loved ones would be doing if they were alive, and what our own role would be. We say things like, "If he were here, we would be planning a second honeymoon." We may remember hopes and dreams for the future more vividly than yesterday's conversations or visitors, and see with sometimes astonishing clarity the minute details of never-to-be-realized scenarios. Many of us may feel as though we are waiting for those scenarios to become physically realized, or focus on the reality that they never will be realized.

Emma said, "If Matt was still alive, what would life be like now? Would he and I still be in a power struggle? Would we still be fighting? Would he be doing well at school? Would he still be with his girlfriend? What music would he be into now? Would he have been annoyed with his little brother trying so hard to be like him, or would he still be so proud? Would he be wanting space from his Mum? Would his voice be starting to break? What would the cool sayings be? Would I still be a cool Mum in his eyes, or would I just be the 'old lady' who keeps grounding him? What clothes would he be bugging me to buy him? Would he be taller than me by now? I hate the what-if's and what-would-be's. I hate reality. I hate that I have been put into a space that I don't want to be in."

As we talked about in the Loss stage, one reason we get angry is because we feel powerless and are trying to feel powerful, to get energy from an external source. How we get that energy is a key to how we deal with this phase. We need to find ways to generate our own energy. As we go through the grief process, we can learn to generate the energy we need by taking care of ourselves physically, nurturing ourselves, and engaging in activities that are energizing (those activities which are not necessarily easy or relaxing – although they may be – but which make us feel better after we do them than we did before we did them). Learning to generate our own energy, depending less on obtaining it from others, can help us become more whole and less needy. But we do not grieve in a vacuum, and our family system plays an increasingly important role as our identity begins to change.

Like adolescents coming home from being away at camp or college, we want to be able to change but not have anything else change while we are gone. But the reality is that our family system often resists our changing. And often, so do we. Think about a college freshman who leaves home and starts to drink excessively in an attempt to soothe his or her anxiety, freeze, and keep things the same. And think about the family system that insists on continuing to treat that college freshman like a child. The effort it takes to change a family system when one of its members begins to change may seem so overwhelming and anxiety-provoking that it seems easier to resist the change.

Conceptualizing the family as a system can help us to understand how all of the members of a family play their part in sustaining the equilibrium of the system. The basic concepts behind Systems Theory are as follows:

1. Wholeness: the whole is greater than the sum of its parts. We cannot understand one part of a system without understanding how it relates to the whole. A family is not a collection of individuals, but a unit made up of individuals, and, at the same time, its own entity. We cannot understand an individual family member without understanding how she or he relates to the whole. A

change in one part of a system will change the system. When one family member changes, the whole system changes.

2. Feedback: is the means of communication, and it is circular, nonlinear. Negative feedback seeks to maintain the status quo, keep the system in balance, or put it back on track. Positive feedback leads to change, introduces new information into the system which is accepted, and unbalances the system. Both types are necessary to sustain a healthy system.

3. Homeostasis: the system tends to regulate itself in order to maintain stability. Family members will attempt to restore a stable environment when it is disrupted, and restrict the range of behavior (breaking up physical fights between sibs). Couples typically begin a relationship with an exuberant, creative, and wide range of behaviors, which gradually narrows to a comfortable, predictable range. Extreme deviation is not desirable! Perhaps when we feel we know someone well, what we really mean is that we know the dynamics of the relationship well – that it has settled down into a predictable pattern.

So, the confusion and uncertainty that we feel in this phase of the grief process is often complicated by the reactions of family and friends to our struggle with expressing the first sprouts of our new identity – far from fully formed at this point, but present and noticeable to those who thought they knew us intimately. Our first faltering steps toward our future identity are often blocked and frustrated by those who become afraid, angry, and bewildered by the person they thought they knew who is now behaving in an unfamiliar manner. A readjustment of the whole family system is sometimes necessary, and strongly resisted by those who felt comfortable – or comfortably familiar – with the way things were before and still perceive themselves in those terms. Paradoxically, the reactions of those around us affirm that we are, indeed, changing and can give us the hopeful sense of moving forward – or, at least, of moving. But those same reactions can be a frightening side effect of the change process, and some of us become so afraid of losing the support we need that we suppress our own growth for the sake of maintaining the status quo. The price we risk paying for this is our own spiritual, physical, and emotional well-being.

"The merry-go-round is going round and round faster and faster," Emily said. "I am standing here looking at it trying to figure out how to get on. If I walk away, I leave my friends and family going round without me, arms outstretched, saying, 'Come on, you can do it.' But a part of me wants to walk away, be alone, and just be. Another part of me wants to grab their outstretched

hands and get back on. Yet it looks so fast, so scary that I am afraid I will either fly off and be hurt or get sick while I am on it. So I just stand here looking. It feels like everyone I love and care for is there and I do not want to be all alone. I have lost so much, I don't want to lose anymore.

"The bills are still coming in, we still need to buy groceries, work at jobs, make the house payment, etc., etc. It doesn't feel like an option to just be in the real world. I feel trapped between not caring about these things anymore and yet knowing that if I don't then my husband has the full burden for this and that isn't fair to him, either. So I am trying to get back on the merry-go-round but can't seem to find a way that will keep me safe.

"I feel caught between the world of grief and the world of healing. And quite frankly I do not know how to go on in this world today. I am not who I was 14 months ago. Yet the world is calling me back. A part of me wants to rejoin the world and a part of me longs to just continue to pull the blanket of grief over me and stay hidden from the world. In some ways it is easier. Although the core of me has not changed, the depth and breadth of who I am has changed dramatically! What does this mean? I wish I knew. I still have many questions and not very many answers. I am finding it very terrifying. I no longer have the energy to be anything but real. So I have been

venturing more and more into this foreign territory of being real wherever I go and whomever I am with, and I am hoping and praying that the long-term outcome will be worth the fears I am now facing. I want to be much more than a survivor. I want to live fully and deeply."

Miya said, "It's now been almost 5 months since my dad passed. My family is feeling very threatened by my new ventures into spirituality and I was accused earlier today of becoming a totally different person 'since grandpa died.' If that's true, then I'm not only different, (I said, 'You bet, I'm different'), I'm better and stronger. They don't like it, my husband and daughter, cause I don't just keep my mouth shut anymore. When I don't like something I say it. I express my opinion. They just didn't listen before so I had stopped talking.

"I've had trouble sleeping recently but I know it's due to my diet and new vitamin regime. Housework's just not that important anymore. Not that the house is dirty, but Martha Stewart is not welcome here, and neither is Julia Child – unless she wants to cook dinner for me. I'm also reading books, visiting websites, taking better care of me. I was so stressed in the 3 months surrounding my dad's passing that I was always sick and my skin was actually peeling off my face, which made me look and feel like an old lady."

We may find ourselves feeling rage or a sense of helpless frustration with those who we perceive as resenting our efforts to express our new identity. After all, there is nothing we can do about the fact that our lives have been unalterably changed!

Griever's Toolbox:

★ Be patient with your need to talk or write about what will never be in the future.

★ Explore feelings of powerlessness.

★ Be aware that as you continue to change, you may experience anxiety over the possible loss of support of family and friends.

★ Safely vent your anger at your own lack of power to prevent life from changing.

★ Keep an Energy Focus journal. Focusing on energy is key when dealing with anger (see Appendix A).

Counseling Interventions:

★ Facilitate the griever's grieving her own lost identity.

★ Educate the griever about family systems. Normalize the fear, anger, and confusion of others as the griever changes. Refer to family counseling if indicated.

Chapter 10
Bargaining

That sense of utter powerlessness in the face of an altered identity can, and often does, again lead grievers back into guilt. We may try desperately to be as we were before, exhausting ourselves in the process. Looking back at who we were, we may feel as though we had forgotten our lines in this life-play. Confronted with the needs of people we love, and recalling the person we wanted to be in relationship to them, we will often strain mightily to remember our lines and act out our part – all the while feeling that we are not, somehow, in character anymore. We may feel we have let others down; have broken some sort of unspoken contract to be someone we can be no longer.

Emily said, "Why can't we just be real? Not everywhere with everyone of course, but much much more and especially with family and friends? I am wondering, if we are more real would others be also? I am wondering why we must wear our masks so much? What are we afraid of? What will happen? I do not have the energy for the mask much anymore. What I am finding is that those who truly care are with me even more deeply, and those who do not care are gone and it's ok. For me real isn't just sharing my pain, but sharing my joy also. Actually it is almost harder to share the joy (even with myself) than the pain as the pain feels more 'acceptable' for a grieving mom. After all, wouldn't I be a much more loving mom if I were in deep pain all the time? O yes, for me it takes much more courage to share my joy! And yet the more real I become the more real people I find to share my real life with.

"I think a lot of why we do this is because we care for people – that we want to wear this mask and spare them the pain that they know we feel. I think what we have to be careful of is always doing this. As I think keeping our masks on with safe people at safe times can stop us from becoming closer to each other and receiving the comfort and caring we need to heal. This is a time to be self-caring, self-focused, and not worry so much about others right now; but it is because we care so much that we do this. But sometimes it is also because we are afraid to see who we are, and let others see who we are, without our masks on.

"I want so badly for someone to take care of me, to help me figure out how to continue on. Today I feel like a failure in every area of my life. I am sorry but I am so tired. Why o why do we torture ourselves so? I think it is

so hard on me because I'm used to being able to be all things to all people.

"I just could not do anything for anyone yesterday, so I didn't. I curled up in bed for a couple of hours, then got up took a shower, and went to my favorite coffee house and picked up a cup of iced tea (peach and ginger, yummy) and went to the public gardens and sat for over 2 hours. When Jack got home I was peaceful, but our house was a mess and there was no dinner. I made no apologies at all. But he knows and he understands, or at least accepts. The one who has trouble understanding, accepting, and letting me off the hook is me!

"I find it very exhausting to have company for long or to be company for long. It takes so much energy to be with others if I feel I must keep on the 'mask' for much of the time. I am going to try experimenting with being less wonderful with others and being more real. Very scary stuff, but it just takes too much energy to try to be who I once was and will never be again, at least not in the same way."

We may take responsibility for the relational chaos of those close to us because it gives us the illusion of having control over that which we are powerless to remedy.

Mark said his wife told him, "You aren't the person I

know," and he replied, "Perhaps he is gone." Then he became teary and I asked if he was grieving the loss of the man who was Nadia's husband. "It's my fault he's gone," Mark said, "I took her husband away. But I can't and won't go back. You can't play a game if you're afraid of losing, because you are going to lose."

When we feel guilty, the question we need to ask is, "What's the fear?" And at this phase, the answer is usually loss of approval and support. And deeper yet than that lies the paralyzing fear of losing whatever stability is left in our world. Perhaps we also fear the loss of who we used to be with our loved one, even if we were not as wise or whole or understanding.

One of the hallmarks of this phase is that we are often extremely hard on ourselves, which brings up the issue of forgiveness. What is forgiveness? Again, it is about letting go of control. Can we let our journey be our own, and let others' be their own? Can we perceive the actions and reactions of others as part of their own journey, and not ours? Can we be ourselves – our changed selves – and let go of the outcome? Can we accept who we are now and share who we are now with those we love? These are questions that can help steer us away from guilt and towards discovering new ways to be and relate.

One of the other fundamental realities that we are

powerless to remedy is the fact that we have become not only changed, but also better and stronger since the death of our loved one. Surviving and navigating the turbulent waters of change frequently opens up fields of thought, emotion, and experience that were previously closed off. Something has begun to fill Circle #2 and give us a glimpse into our new world. Grievers often feel a new sense of connection with the universal rhythm of the cycle of life and death, a new appreciation for the beauty and lessons of nature, and a new empathy with others who suffer. We typically say things at this point such as, "I'm a better person now." And yet the pull backwards is often still very strong. It may sometimes feel tempting to stop the process and keep our focus on the past, the known, the familiar.

This brings up complex feelings about who we were before. Some of us dwell on regrets for lost opportunities with our loved one. We replay scenes from the past in our minds and rewrite the scenes so the outcome seems more favorable, or reflects our better self.

Mark described the ways in which he has reached out to others who have had losses, addictions, and depression. He was active in many ways – politically and privately – and sharing his experience had given him great satisfaction and helped him heal. Then he said tearfully, "I wish I'd known sooner what I was doing to myself. Maybe the grieving process would have been easier, or at least over sooner. When you start drinking, you freeze."

In the Loss stage, we wait for our deceased loved ones to be restored; in the Return stage we wait for our living family members and friends to catch up – to perceive the world through our new eyes. As we tentatively begin to form our new identities we may, like adolescents, focus on those around us who have not changed. "I seem to be so far ahead of them. Why can't they change as I have?" grievers are likely to ask the counselor in disillusioned frustration. We often feel puzzled and disappointed when others respond to us with the same sympathetic words and looks as they did immediately following our loss. We may find ourselves trying relentlessly to explain ourselves and convince others that we have found a better way to be, and we have trouble understanding responses that are not positive or encouraging. Alternatively, we may resist facing reality and convince ourselves that our friends and loved ones have indeed changed, or are on the brink of seeing the light. The underlying need here is for approval and support; and deeper yet than that lies the paralyzing fear of losing whatever stability is left in our world.

Amy talked about how she had grown through her

grief process. "I've survived it and I've learned a lot. My mom just doesn't get it. What makes me mad is that she treats me like I'd fall apart if you blew on me. She won't even talk about it. Doesn't she see I won't break? I try to tell her but she looks at me like it doesn't compute or something. I know that's because she won't deal with her own issues. If I can do it, why can't everyone?"

Julia, 47, whose sister died a year earlier, said, "My family acts like nothing is wrong. This afternoon I just lost it with them and said, 'I can't pretend with you anymore! My life is not the same and it never will be again!' Now I feel guilty and worn out. I am tired of grieving alone. Sometimes I just want to stop all the avoidance and force them to face this! I wish I knew what to do. They make me feel like my grieving is somehow wrong, and they don't see that I'm the only one who's really dealing with it."

Griever's Toolbox:

★ Explore feelings of guilt about not being the same person, causing others' loss.

★ Use this metaphor: The mask. Explore the advantages and disadvantages of keeping it on.

★ Continue to process the sorting out of elements of your past and present identity.

★ Self-exploration, self-care, and self-focus.

★ Continue to focus on what has been learned, and on how you have grown.

★ If you need to, express your regret over lost opportunities with the loved one.

★ Draw a time line of your life and indicate 5 or 6 major turning points. Then identify the circumstances that preceded those turning points. Most turning points are preceded by a crisis, major change, or situation perceived at the time as negative. See the connection between the crises and positive turning points.

★ Let go of trying to "help" family and/or friends change, or of the expectation that they will.

★ Find new friends who share your present interests or direction. Pay attention to who appears.

★ Learn about the next phase of the grief process and what to expect.

Counseling Interventions:

★ Compare this phase to adolescence.
★ Address the griever's deep fears of losing whatever stability is left in his world.

Chapter 11
Depression

This is the dark night of the soul. It may be the most difficult and painful phase of the grief process, and it often occurs between 18 and 24 months after the death. It is when we begin to clearly comprehend the fact that we are not the same person we were when our loved one died. The distance in time and space and experience between us and our loved one seems like a chasm too wide to bridge, and at the same time, we are almost unrecognizable to ourselves. Our anxious attempts to be who we were in the past slide down the walls of that chasm, and a sense of profound sadness and resignation takes their place. We may feel we have no control over anything at all; and, at the same time, we are struggling awkwardly with letting go of the guilt, anger, and fear that have held us back. We may sense how far we have come, and at the same time sense we have not gone far enough and have no inner compass to guide us through the confusing maze of paths that lies ahead. We may feel vulnerable, unprotected, defenseless. Some of us know, some suspect, some doubt, and many resist the fact that letting go completely of the attempt to control the process will lead us toward the gains that will balance the losses.

Julia said, "I think I thought if I did all the right things, I wouldn't end up in this place of deep depression. Well I guess being smart is no match for grief. I am trying to be patient, although right now I just don't give a damn. I am so tired of this pain, this life. I am so completely void of any life on the inside. I am alive in the physical sense, but that is all. And yet it is as though no one out there can even tell. I must be a pretty good actress. Or maybe they just don't want to see. Whatever. I have run out of answers and I have run out of caring about finding them. Is it letting go or giving up?"

At this point, we often withdraw from social contact unrelated to our loss. Many of us find that the idle chit-chat, small talk, and gossip that we used to indulge in enthusiastically is not only unfulfilling, but irritating. We have no energy to waste on anything unrelated to our grief, and we struggle to focus on getting our psychic bearings in our changed world. I have found that this withdrawal often signals the first step toward redefining identity. If we can recognize the necessity to be consciously aware of how and where our limited energies are directed, we become therapeutically and appropriately as self-centered as infants – which also means as open to possibilities. And although we often feel as though our lives are over (and indeed they are over as they once were) we are taking the first tentative, toddling steps toward beginning again. But this time, instead of growing up through dependence on a family, we need to grow up apart from everyone else – to rebirth ourselves.

Amy said she had been crying uncontrollably for the past few weeks and did not understand why. "I feel burned out," she said, "but I know I don't have a choice. I gotta go forward. I feel like I'm 17 again and I hate it . . . and I already know you can't go back."

Complicating the confusion of our mood is the sense we often have of having gone backwards in the process, and thus of having failed. The profound sadness that we experience again, after having survived it in the Loss stage with a new knowledge of our own strength, may make us doubt that strength is a real and permanent part of our identity. We may think we had been fooling ourselves, and despair of ever achieving a sustained sense of peace and wholeness.

Mark was feeling as though the past was close around him. He recently spoke at a forum on depression, which was satisfying but at the same time brought feelings back from his depression of the previous year and left him emotionally exhausted and drained. Talking to a friend about "past escapades and foibles that took me back to the past didn't feel too good." Baseball season had just started, and that again brought his thoughts back to the past and to his father. Their mutual love for baseball had been one of their strongest connections.

Mark had moved out of his house and said, "I've been thinking about going back to be with my kids, but it's just a feeling. To throw away all I've gone through, to walk back through those doors would freeze the process all over again. But sometimes I wonder how far I've come. A lot of people think I'm regressing. When do you quit having to revisit the past?" I said, "You never go back to exactly the same place. You revisit it from a different perspective. And each time you go back a little bit you learn something else." "That is certainly true," Mark said. "I've learned you can change the past as the time of being the changed 'you' lengthens and begins to balance the old. You see the past more clearly. Sometimes I'm shocked to find out how wrong my perceptions were . . . how things I thought were insurmountable and unforgivable aren't even remembered by others. I wasted so many years, but I was able to accomplish a lot, even in the grip of a disease I had no idea I had. I survived. That's the miracle. But sometimes I feel overwhelmed. It's like I'm a TV picture slowly blacking out – I'm disappearing and I can't get myself back."

Self-doubt, combined with an aching feeling of loss and fear of the unknown future, makes this phase one during which support and the instillation of hope are most essential. We often feel as though our world and our identity are up for grabs and we don't have the emotional, physical, or psychic resources to reconstruct either of them. And yet, paradoxically, the self-doubt we experience here is the doorway to the very future we simultaneously yearn for and fear. We often seem to doubt everything we had taken for granted and all we had valued, and that is desirable. If we tried to exist in the new situation without change, we would deny the loss and hence the prior value. To doubt the whole of existence is a prelude to moving fully into the new world beyond the loss. This is the beginning of the ending that leads to the beginning, for we must lose our life in order to find it. Some grievers reflect on a sense of surprise that they could simultaneously lose their lives and continue living, and that surprise can demonstrate to them that they are, indeed, stronger than they suspected. They begin to realize that they can let go, and that going back to their lives as they were is not an option.

Charles, a 60-year-old widower whose wife had died 3 years before, told me of a wonderful Mary Engelbreit print that was meaningful to him. It had the words "Don't Look Back" at the top. The drawing was of a crossroads. In one direction was a sign that read "Your Future;" in the other direction one that read, "Not an Option." He said, "As much as I miss the life we shared when she was physical, I can't go back. It's not an option. That road is closed forever and I can only go in the other direction. What is down that road is yet for me to discover, and I have to give myself permission and the time and space and opportunity to do that or I'll remain stuck at the crossroads. I could stay still but I would spend the rest of my life looking back, trying to find sustenance from the ghostly forms of what has been. There is something so seductive and romantic in the idea of living that kind of existence. For me that doesn't seem to be an option."

I am reminded of the movie *The Fisher King*. Both of the main characters, when they experienced a loss, had to let go of their entire lives and start all over again in order to heal. And escaping the pain did not work. The Grail was beyond the grasp of people avoiding reality. It can be healing to use myth, fantasy, and metaphor as a way to structure the reconstruction of identity.

Like the characters in *The Fisher King*, we need to let

go of our life as it is in order to move on. As long as we hold onto who we were in the past, we will not be able to let go of what our relationship with our loved one was. We need to figure out who we are apart from everyone else, apart from the old us.

Mark mentioned Parsifal and the Grail quest. I asked him, "What's your Grail?" "I don't know," he replied. "I thought it was them. I think my Grail has something to do with my father . . . perhaps Our Father. The Tao Te Ching says you have to open yourself before the flow can come in – empty yourself to be full. I don't know if I'm empty yet, but I'm getting in the red part of the fuel gauge." I asked him to think about the Grail quest without relation to anyone but himself. "I would like to feel part of the human race," he replied, "and not apart from . . . connected." I responded that he was starting to focus more on himself and seemed less distrustful of his feelings. "I've always had the courage to learn and make mistakes," he said. "I don't believe anymore that I can't do things."

Many of us feel as though our soul will always have holes in it like a moth-eaten quilt. But, to hope that fulfillment can be found even through the holes; to engage in the process of revealing within our changed selves the links to what the forever-changed world outside ourselves is presenting is the process of making a connection that can lead toward our own resurrection.

Mark was feeling tense, sad, and irritable on Easter Sunday. He questioned himself about why he felt so sad when others in his family that he loved seemed to be doing ok without his presence. "The answer was 'because you're a miserable bastard and you want everyone to be miserable with you,' " he said. I remarked that he seemed to be beating himself up. He said, "I don't think these feelings are something I can control, but I think I have a rudimentary understanding of what they are . . . sometimes I don't know what they are, and it's a little scary." I suggested that when something scares us we try to take control by feeling guilty and blaming ourselves, when what happened was a normal grieving over the loss of his family being together at Easter. "That sounds pretty good," he said. Mark then went on to talk about his dad, who had never supported him. "Quit being a dumbass, he would say. But I couldn't quit being a dumbass because the things he thought I was being a dumbass about were these feelings I have that are very useful and helpful for me today."

During this phase of the process, I had a dream that I

gave birth to a baby, and when I looked at it, it was me. Many other grievers have told me they had that same dream. We who are at this step need to get in touch with the child inside in order to grow from there into who we will be. Actually, we need to be as self-centered as an infant. To separate our identity from that of our loved one we need to accept the person we are now, apart from any other relationship.

There is a wonderful illustration of this step in the movie *Forrest Gump*. After his mother dies and Jenny leaves him yet again, Forrest starts to run. He stops to eat when he is hungry and to sleep when he is tired. He runs just because that is what he feels like doing, and in the process he begins to let go of the past and get in touch with who he is.

Following our impulses is one way to learn about who we are now. There was a playground near my house in Virginia, and I used to drive past it almost every day. After my daughter died, I began to feel pulled toward it when I drove by. I felt the urge to go and play there, but always resisted it. Then one day I stopped resisting, drove into the parking lot, got out of my car, and played on the swings. It felt wonderfully liberating and energizing! I realized later that that impulse had been telling me that I needed to get back in touch with myself as a child – not the child I used to be, but the child of who I am now. I learned to trust those kinds of impulses because they always led me to an awareness I would not have gained by simply thinking about or analyzing my feelings. Sometimes acting out can lead to learning.

Emily told a wonderful story of healing: "Yesterday I woke up and the old familiar exhaustion and pain was there and I felt tired. Then I remembered the very wise advice you gave me of treating myself like a 'self-indulgent baby.' So, I actually went shopping and bought baby products to use – baby lotion, baby bath, etc. I have always loved the smell of this stuff. I also sprinkled baby powder on my sheets before I went to bed last night and I had the best night's sleep I have had in a long time. I also bought some 50s rock and roll music – something I love but have not even been able to listen to since Megan died. My Megan was always a dancer, literally and figuratively. And the message I have been receiving from the universe this week is dance!' So I put on my '50s music and I danced to "Runaround Sue," "The Lion Sleeps Tonight," "Chantilly Lace," "Louie Louie," and lots more. I just kept dancing and singing and I swear I could hear Megan almost doubled over in laughter at her silly mother. And as I was dancing the sun came out! I swear! Now this is major as we have had almost no sun in 18 days! And I feel closer to Megan than I have felt for a long time! Then I took a shower and used some of my baby lotion and then I had a reflexology treatment and indulged in a chocolate brownie at my favorite coffee bar. O yes, I feel better!"

The Accidental Tourist

The film *The Accidental Tourist* is a moving and accurate presentation of the complex emotions of the Return stage - especially the Depression and Acceptance phases. When Macon Leary's son Ethan dies, he tries to stay the same while the world changes around him. A travel writer, his logo is a traveling armchair, and his motto is: "While armchair travelers dream of going places, traveling armchairs dream of staying put." A fan tells him that traveling with the Accidental Tourist is "like traveling in a cocoon, you never feel like you've left home." Macon goes to Paris and eats at Burger King. We can tell that his story is about the Return stage because he focuses less on the loss of his son than on his own identity and his confusion about what exactly that is. Does he want to follow his family traditions and go back to live in his childhood home, stay in his marriage, get a divorce, begin a new relationship, live with his new love Muriel or marry her, stay in the "Leary groove" or move out of it and move forward.

We watch Macon Leary go through Denial. He has

trouble making decisions, so he lets Muriel make them. He tries to keep going in the same way, in the same old behavior patterns, and he focuses on keeping busy. He is drawn to new things, but he pulls back.

We see him in the Anger phase when he has an accident in his basement and has to deal with his dog Edward (who expresses his repressed anger) biting people. He senses himself going backwards, and in a pivotal scene, he tells Muriel: "Every day I tell myself it's time to be getting over this. I know that people expect it of me. But if anything, I'm getting worse. The first year was like a bad dream. I was clear to his door in the morning before I remembered he wasn't there to be wakened. But the second year is real. I've stopped going to his door, I've sometimes let a whole day pass by without thinking about him. I believe Sarah thinks I could have prevented what happened somehow. She's so used to my arranging her life. Now I'm far from everyone. I don't have any friends anymore. And everyone looks trivial and foolish and not related to me."

He has changed, and yet he feels powerless to change, and can't let go of control. And his family system resists his changing and tried to pull him back into their old familiar behavior patterns.

Then Macon goes through the Bargaining phase. He puts on his mask and goes back to Sarah, allowing her to take control of his life because he feels guilty that he did not do it right the first time. But he comes to the realization that he feels better about himself with Muriel and she, not knowing that but knowing he needs her, goes to Paris on the same plane. In Paris, he is about to invite her to go on a trip with him, when he again hurts his back. The back symbolizes the heart. Macon is afraid of losing the last vestiges of stability and support he thinks he has.

Macon shows us the Depression phase (and when you see this film, you will notice that he does not experience the phases in a linear fashion) when he regresses. When he fears a loss of support, he goes back to his family and his childhood home, withdraws from social contacts, doesn't answer the phone, feels vulnerable and refuses to eat the turkey his sister makes on Thanksgiving because he thinks it's undercooked and dangerous. When his family criticizes his new relationship with Muriel, he gives up and goes back to Sarah.

Finally, if the Acceptance phase can be called a "happy ending," that's what we get at the end of this film. Macon chooses to move forward into a new life after being in the foreign city of Paris. He has realized that losing his life is finding it, and he reconnects with Muriel. When he does that, he also reconnects with Ethan in a new way, and in the last scene we see that he comes to understand that Ethan will always be there, and that Macon has learned what is essential and leaves all his *baggage* behind, except for Ethan's photograph. At last, he gives up trying to control life and takes control of his own life.

Griever's Toolbox:

★ Acknowledge this as the worst point in the grief process, and give yourself credit for being courageous enough to deal with it.

★ Use this metaphor: The chasm between you and your loved one plus the chasm between your past and present identity seem too wide to bridge.

★ Explore your feelings of being vulnerable, unprotected, and defenseless.

★ Let go of attempting to control the process. If you cannot let go on your own, seek professional support.

★ Engage in infantile self-centeredness.

★ Monitor your energy level and engage in enjoyable activities.

★ Understand that your self-doubt, sense of regression, disappointment in not being farther along in the process, sense of failure, and fear of the unknown future are all normal at this phase and are not permanent.

★ Reframe your doubt of self and world as the doorway to the future. We must lose our lives in order to find them, and you are strong enough to lose your life and continue living.

★ Use this metaphor: You stand at a crossroads. A sign pointing one way says "Your life." A sign pointing the other way says, "No longer an option." There is a Mary

Engelbreit print of this image, available on her website. Get it if you can. Set up a tent at the crossroads until you feel ready to move on.

★ View the film *The Fisher King*. Focus on the themes of grief, the Grail Quest, and transformation.

★ Act on your impulses as a way toward healing and self-discovery.

Counseling Interventions:

★ Educate the griever about why this is happening and reframe it in a positive and hopeful way.

★ Instill hope at every opportunity.

★ Anticipate the griever's withdrawal from social contacts. Reframe that withdrawal as a positive and necessary step toward redefining her identity.

★ Keep the therapeutic focus on the griever.

★ Validate the griever's feeling that her life is over (life as it *was* is over) and the arduous task she now has of rebirthing herself.

★ Therapist support is more crucial here than at any other point. Be available. But remember, you also need to let go and let the griever experience this in her own way.

Chapter 12
Acceptance

The acceptance of the Return stage is more complex than that of the Loss stage. It requires a simultaneous letting go and moving forward. At this point we have left behind who we were in the past, have accepted our changed identity, and now need to discover what exactly that means. Acceptance does not mean the end of sadness. The sense of loss and the aching for a future that will never be may still be acute. But most of us feel an exhilaration of moving ahead in the process that is often tempered by the seemingly daunting task that lies before us of recreating ourselves. Paradoxically, part of that recreation involves the ability to forget our loved one once in a while. When we begin to focus on living rather than on remembering, we remember our loved one in everything we do. At this step we learn that control is an illusion and learning to focus our energy and letting go with hope is the mechanism that leads us forward.

Martha said she did not understand how her feelings could change so much from day to day. Sometimes she did not think about Jessica at all, and then she wondered if she was forgetting her and felt guilty about it. I asked her if, when Jessica was alive, she had to think about her every minute to know she was a part of her life and that she loved her. Martha responded, "No . . . I had to start all over. You won't ever leave her, but you have to make these steps without her . . . but it's not without her because she's there!" Then Martha talked about how she had started living more in the present, like Jessica did. She was beginning to enjoy life instead of constantly planning for the future. "Jessica was so much like me," Martha remarked. "And I didn't see it back then."

It can be painful for grievers to admit to themselves that they are strengthened and enhanced because their loved one has died. A healing reframe of this reality from a spiritual perspective is that when people progress and learn through the grief process, their loved ones are also helped to progress, and freed to learn without feeling called to try to comfort those who are grieving and help them survive their derangement.

Chloe said, "I'm letting go slowly but surely, but it feels weird. I have to learn to see through my own eyes. I felt like I had to keep earning my dad's love by giving my life force to him. Now I realize that all that does is take away from me. I know I have no control over it, but at the same time I shouldn't let it control me. All I can control is my own choices. In a way it's a relief, because I feel I don't have to control every little aspect. Instead of dwelling on what I can't change I need to build on it from where I am now. I've been living my life to try to keep people from leaving me the way my dad did. I'm in control of me now. That's real different. I don't feel so helpless. I don't feel I have no control over what goes on in my life." I said what I was hearing was that by letting go, Chloe felt as though she was more in control. "Yes," she replied, "I'm going to do stuff and see what happens."

Mark said, "Nadia is never going to know who I am. I'm not her husband. 'That's not true,' she says. That's her answer to everything I say about how I feel: 'That's not true.' I wonder if I'll ever be able to have a normal relationship or will I end up alone. I don't beat myself up as much anymore because I was just trying to be what everyone wanted me to be. My dad wanted me to be what he couldn't be. And I set these lofty goals and kept falling short."

Taking our first faltering steps toward a future identity we can only guess at, we often become self-absorbed and may appear egocentric. Fascinated with and totally immersed in the process of self-discovery, our attention span may seem short and our memory impaired when it is focused outside ourselves. It is important that counselors encourage this self-absorption and self-exploration. Asking grievers at this step to think about how others feel, or to consider adjusting their behavior to make others less uncomfortable is counterproductive.

Mark realized that Nadia was not dealing with her role in their problems. "To this day," he said, "she persists in saying 'I had no part in this. I feel helpless and abandoned.' And I want to scream at her, 'Have you ever explored any of your own part in this?' I've seen a lot of people do the same thing and never get over it. I've been real close to going back, but I refuse to be 'miserable and happy' so they can feel good. Every time I have those feelings I'll go back, something graphically reminds me of what it was like, what happened, and what it's like now. And I've learned that it's not what's 'true' that matters, but what is true and real from someone's perspective."

Emily said, "We may feel like we are 'dying' when we first begin to face this and in a sense we are. Our old life, old way of being, is gone forever and so we must not only grieve the loss of our precious children on this earth but we must also grieve the loss of our lives as they once were. No wonder it is so scary! This is the biggest,

greatest loss anyone can ever experience! We also cannot
face this darkness alone. That is why God gave us each
other."

What if we did not accept and reform our identity?
What would that look like? How can we recognize it when
we or others are stuck? Essentially, not accepting means
finding a way to freeze ourselves. People, being extremely
inventive, do that in many ways: self-medication,
addiction to shopping or gambling or food or one of
thousands of other activities or substances, stunting their
own growth by contracting the scope of their world and
limiting the range of their interactions with it, or focusing
exclusively on their loved one's life. That is what the fear of
letting go looks like. We focus on control, and give up our
own future for the sake of holding onto the past.

Letting go of trying to control the process – letting go
of trying to reach across that chasm and bring the past into
the present – makes energy available for moving into the
future. Energy focused on the future is available when we
get there. So, throughout the grief process, the more we
can focus on the future, the easier it will be to discover
what it holds for us, and the more fullness we are likely to
find when we get there.

The struggle to form a new identity has to do with

focusing the energy released through the process of accepting the change. We who reach this point – and not everyone does – have let go of the anxiety that kept us focused on trying to control the released energy, and have also let go of the depression that kept us focused on our inability to control that energy. What we now discover is a perception of ourselves that is at once familiar, different, and incomplete. We have the same skills, abilities, knowledge, appearance (although it may have changed somewhat), and experiences as we did before – and those aspects of our identities are familiar. But we also have discovered aspects that are different – that have changed since the loss. What used to seem important often seems trivial and superficial, and what was barely paid attention to before seems of the highest value and meaning. For example, in the past we may have focused on success and the acquisition of material things. After experiencing the loss and coming to the realization that physical reality is fragile and transient, our priorities are reordered and we often see more value in relationships and connections and spirituality. The recognition of these differences in perception that began in the Loss stage is acted upon in the Return stage.

George had been out of work (by his own choice) for a while. He had been thinking about going back to his old job, mainly because he felt competent there and it paid well, but now he was thinking about doing something new and responded positively when I suggested career counseling. He was also looking toward selling his parents' house and thinking about getting married and having a child. "I might as well change everything!" he said. He was making new friends and playing golf with "a nice group of guys." Like his dad he had always had many casual acquaintances but not many close friends. Now he was expanding his horizons. He had changed the way he interacted with people, he said. "Now I relate on a deeper, more feeling level. I tell people I'm not working because of my parents' deaths and I hear others' stories. I'm helping a friend of mine deal with his grief, and that feels good. I have more self-esteem, I trust myself more, and I'm more loving."

What is incomplete at this phase is our ability to express our new perceptions within the new context of our lives. The future can no longer be viewed as a known quantity, or as a function of the simple anticipation of an automatic effect that can be triggered by putting into motion a reliable cause. *Result B* does not necessarily follow from *Action A* anymore.

"I'm seeing a lot of changes," Amy said, "and it's a

*little scary. Even Martin said he sees the changes in me.
I'm more cool and calm. I'm afraid my marriage may
suffer because I've changed so much. Martin didn't want
me to talk to you about James because it was too
upsetting. Now he's surprised at how far I've come. I
guess I finally feel like I've got paddles in my hands for
the boat."*

At the beginning of this phase, we do not always know
how we will respond to something or what we want. We
express uncertainty about taking a specific course of action
because we have little sense of how meaningful or fulfilling
it will be for us. One client of mine at this step said she was
reluctant to try new behaviors because they "felt fake."

Learning theory gives us a useful concept for
understanding the process of changing thoughts and
behaviors: *Cognitive dissonance.* It can be defined as a
state of discomfort that arises when we find ourselves
acting or thinking in ways that do not seem to fit with our
customary behaviors. New behaviors can feel "fake" and
uncomfortable at first, and that does not mean they are
not genuine – it just means they are new.

So, an integral part of this step is the learning to do it
anyway – to do something in order to *find out* whether it
will be fulfilling. Something helpful to do is change with
control – change any small thing one can think of and see

what happens. This gives us both a sense of having some control over change, and a nonthreatening way to discover new things that may become part of our new identity.

The necessity of acting in this manner – which is often very different from familiar behavior patterns – and the hope that there are rewards and meaning to be found in the process is what moves us forward to try new things and to find new *foci* for our undifferentiated energies. It is hope that drives the change process. as Vaclav Havel said so eloquently, hope "transcends the world that is immediately experienced and is anchored somewhere beyond its horizon . . . It is not the conviction that something will turn out well, but the certainty that something makes sense regardless of how it turns out. It is hope above all which gives us the strength to live and try new things."

Chloe said, "I have more hope now than I did. I've let go of trying to make things turn out the 'right' way. I might go back to school, but right now I'm taking a rest from feeling needed. I need me, too. I need to recharge, be lazy, read. It feels good to take control . . . weird, but good. I feel stronger . . . I feel it here [pointing to her midsection.] It feels good. I always had good instincts but I didn't listen to them. Now I listen."

Hope is the medium of change within perception, the momentum that transforms a belief into a vision. It is a trusting that after the situation we will perceive meaning and learn from it. It does not imply that the death of our loved one was ok by standards of before the event, but it can make meaning of realities. We, through hope, perceive meaning where, without that hope, we would have none; and those perceptions open us to new experiences – to the possibilities we could not see without it.

Mark said, "There's a plan we don't get to see. Life is like a puzzle, and we get one piece a day. Some of the pieces are the pretty light ones we all may want to believe we deserve, and some are the dark ones we question whether we deserve. Faith is believing that the big picture is more light than dark, and I have faith."

Emily said, "For today, I will care for myself because I do not want my children to suffer anymore than they already have; and if I do not care for myself I will have nothing to give them. And in time, I believe and have hope that I too will benefit, and that my life will become filled with life and meaning once again."

As we proceed through the Return stage, we find ourselves being "made new." The best outcome we can wish for here is to stop being afraid of the released energy of change we feel and to begin to sense its presence as exciting opportunities for growth and learning. One good indication that we are, indeed, at this point in the process is the sense of having more energy. Often, this will show in our physical appearance – hair will seem shinier, face will have more color, eyes will be brighter, movements will be more fluid and controlled. Some grievers will start talking about a new career, going back to school, doing volunteer work, or trying out their new identities in new relationships. This can be a time of excitement and challenge.

So, why isn't this the end of the grief process? The answer to that question lies, once again, with the loss. We have experienced a loss that has led us to a changed identity. But since we still miss our loved one and are still feeling the loss, we must find a way to reconnect with that loved one from the perspective of that changed identity – and also from the perspective of the loved one's changed identity. For yes, because and although the loved one is no longer physical, the role she played in our life has changed and we need to find a way to incorporate that change into life and make meaning out of it. Otherwise, we will continue to remember the lost loved one as if she were still physical and frozen in time.

Griever's Toolbox:

★ Monitor your energy level. Look for an increase in energy as an indication of being at this step.

★ Learn and think about the next task of trying out a new identity in a changed world.

★ Do the Then... Now exercise (Appendix A).

★ Gather photos of yourself at different ages. As you look at them, think about your essential self – not the roles you play or your physical characteristics, but about what fulfills and energizes you, what facets of life call to you at the core of your being.

★ Reward yourself for having gotten this far in the process, and for what you have learned. Enumerate all that you have learned so far. Write it down.

★ If you believe in an afterlife, reframe your sense of distance from your loved one as helping your loved one to spiritually progress by letting go.

★ Remind yourself that this is a slow process, composed of infinite tiny steps, and that you are just beginning to learn about who you are now.

★ Recognize that you may seem self-absorbed and egocentric. Your attention span may seem short and memory impaired when focused externally.

★ Explore changed priorities, values, and new ways that you perceive life.

★ Understand that it is normal to feel scared when

dealing with so many changes.
★ Change with control – change any small thing and see what happens.
★ Explore your perception of the meaning of your loss experience.
★ Keep a Gratitude Journal.
★ Ponder the idea of reconnection.

Counseling Interventions:

★ Normalize the griever's ambivalent feelings about letting go and moving forward.
★ Normalize any guilt the griever may feel about sometimes forgetting the loved one.
★ Work with the griever to create his genogram.
★ Educate about learning theory and how new behaviors can feel fake and uncomfortable at first, and that does not mean they are not genuine – it just means they are new.
★ Continue to instill hope. It is the medium of change.

Chapter 13
I'll Cross That Bridge When I Come to It

Most of us are, by this point, aware that our journey – while personal – is not traveled alone. We have lived in many relationships, and now live in many relationships; and the recognition of the change from past to present in each of them now defines the moment. To move further along the path of bereavement without a short, conscious evaluation of what has happened and is happening for us in relationship to others would make what is still to come either impossible or impossibly lonely. So, this phase is a bridge between Return and Reconnection, a breathing space, an assessment.

We often delay dealing with relationship issues until we have some better sense of who we have become, but we need to begin to really deal with it before we can reconnect in all directions. We may not yet know fully who we are, but when we have returned we have a more realistic view of all the *now* and *then* relationships of life and death.

In the Return stage, we return to ourselves as we have become and to ourselves as we were, to others as they are and as they were, and to the lost ones as they have become and as they were. So now it is a 6-sided equation, and more complex because we who have found paths to return must now guide others. So others who are as they are now, but try to think of themselves as they were, must be helped to relate to the lost person as he is now – not as he was – and as the living are now. So a shift may be about changes in as many as 5 dimensions: self now, others now and then, and loved one now and then. And we who get ourselves reconnected often think it is not worth it, because everyone else then seems either out of it or demanding.

We who have accepted our loss and then have accepted our own changed identity are no longer clinging to the past so fervently, and thus are in a position to recognize that shift in ourselves and in others around us. We are more consciously aware of our own strengths and needs, and thus are in a position to communicate them to others around us. We have a better sense of who our loved one was, because we have less of an investment in perceiving her through the distorted lens of our own needs. We may not feel we have total clarity about who we are, but that is not a real issue since the sense of there being more to come is an intrinsic part of the process when we are moving forward. Those who feel they know who they are completely are usually stuck in some way.

Once again, the unknown must be confronted, but this time it is in terms of relationships. Just as our friends and family may resist accepting our changed identity, so we may also resist what can feel like yet another loss – the changing identities of friends and family. We may be unwilling to invest energy in helping others change when we do not know the outcome of that change. Or we may feel inadequate to guide others because of an inability to focus what feels like severely limited energy in that direction. Once again, the familiar may be painful but at least it is known. Or we may try to deny that others need guidance, and may even blame ourselves for problems in relationships.

We are more likely to react to friends and family with anger, frustration, or even guilt, than to reach out in understanding and compassion to share what we have learned along the way thus far. It is simply easier to react than it is to try to consciously devise an approach that will be helpful for both ourselves and each individual in relationship with us. And yet, if this is not accomplished and we continue to react automatically, we may find ourselves without support, which can make the rest of the process very painful or even impossible – and may mean the additional loss of some valued and valuable connections.

Every time we move further along the complexity of

healing, our relationships to others grow more complex – unless the others also move and grow. If everyone is on the same page it gets easier. If not, it gets easier personally and harder interpersonally. So counselors may hear, "I got my act together, so why does this all still seem so hard."

In a society that emphasizes the individual, people often perceive themselves as operating in a kind of vacuum where no one but them is affected by how their life proceeds. In other societies, which emphasize the group, the individual's importance is perceived as its effect on the consensus or harmonious interaction of the group. What both of these perspectives seem to miss is the interconnectedness of all. If I change, then I may lose my current relationships unless they and I perceive us as changing together. And if the group changes, I may lose my sense of self unless it and I perceive us as changing together. An individual cannot be fulfilled apart from a group, and a group cannot be fulfilled apart from the individuals who comprise it. In both types of social orientation, when one individual changes others are affected, and their needs and emotions need to be addressed – not defensively or condescendingly, but in a spirit of partnership and unity and connection.

So, to return from social theory back to the grievers' dilemma, at this phase it will be necessary for us to take a step back and reassess our own process and relationships

– to breathe, to reflect, to contemplate, to ponder. There may be a temptation, for grievers and counselors alike, to keep charging forward – especially when so much progress and discovery is unfolding. But all learnings need time and space to become integrated into a person's being. And a step back can give us the chance to see ourselves and our relationships with greater clarity – and that includes our relationship to our lost loved one.

This Bridge is a moveable and fluid one, and it may appear at many points in the grief process. As is true of all the stages, it may be revisited whenever we sense ourselves as having moved forward beyond our relationships – living or physically dead.

So, this is a place for such questions as:

- What have I learned so far about myself and others?
- How do others perceive me?
- What can I do to help those I am connected with understand me better?
- How can I help them understand any perceived gaps between us?
- Are there any relationships I need to let go?
- What have others been offering me that I have been dismissing, disrespecting, or devaluing?
- How can I be more truly myself in the

relationships I want or need to sustain?

- What am I holding onto that may be interfering with mutual support and understanding?
- How am I behaving differently than I have in the past and what affect is that having on others?
- What do I need from others and what are they saying they need from me?
- Since I am in transition, how can I deal with that and the confusion it elicits in others at the same time?
- Am I focusing on the past, present, or future of my relationships?
- Are there new relationships and connections I need to make?
- What can I share with others that will guide them toward me rather than away from me?

As you may have noticed, these questions are not focused on others, but on *relationship* to others.

Reconnection will be much more problematic if we do not deal with our own connections. If we learn and practice the art of connection, we will be better prepared for the next stage of Reconnection.

Griever's Toolbox:

★ Take a break from dealing with self.

★ Ask yourself what your perception is of how others relate to you, and whether it feels past or present.

★ Communicate clearly to others your strengths and needs. Deal with any anxiety that results from that suggestion. Seek support for this if you need it. Self-assess your communication style (see Appendix A).

★ Explore any anger in relationships.

★ Examine each close relationship to consciously devise an approach that will be helpful, and share what you have learned along the way so far. This is necessary if you are to maintain needed support.

★ Write a Personal Ad (see Appendix A).

Counseling Interventions:

★ Explore any denial about others' need to change in relation to the griever, and/or guilt about the changes being experienced in her relationships.

★ Explore any perceived need the griever has for ending or beginning new relationships.

★ If necessary, teach assertive communication skills.

Stage 3: Reconnection

If I can take the dark with open eyes
And call it seasonal, not harsh or strange
(For love itself may need a time of sleep),
And, treelike, stand unmoved before the change,
Lose what I lose to keep what I can keep,
The strong root still alive under the snow,
Love will endure – if I can let you go.

– May Sarton (from *Autumn Sonnets*)

Chapter 14
Reconnection

If we can let go of the physical, the essential will endure. In the Reconnection stage, your job is to find what persists – what fills the intersection of the 2 circles – so that you can reconnect.

It is especially important to remember that all of the stages, steps, phases, or moods described in this book are interchangeable and nonlinear – not sequential, hierarchical, and invariant stages as we tend to think of them. If I could illustrate the spiral of change as having more than 2 dimensions, you would see that it has depth; and also that its loop is really multiple – even infinite – loops, all intra-connecting and intersecting. In order to understand the change process it is crucial to understand that there is really no regression other than standing still. Any movement on the spiral will lead forward eventually. And if we have tried really hard to stay put, be inert, then freeing up ourselves can be also letting ourselves step back now and then. Sometimes in crossing a mountain we go downhill to find a more possible uphill route. For this reason, it is important for the counselor to meet clients at whatever point they are focusing on and not try to use this theory or any other to superimpose a rigid structure on what is an essentially fluid and multidimensional process. Another important consideration to remember is that often grievers will have one foot on one step and the other foot on another. We will often not be wholly in one stage until we get about halfway along it. And each step may evoke issues from other sub-steps. And some steps are trickier than others, and trickier for some than others. It is harder for a one-legged person to be on multiple steps – which is to say that our psychological complexity will also be a determinant in our ability to creatively deal with the necessary dissonance of the process. But that dissonance at some level must be felt, acknowledged, and lived through to meaning; for it is the very seeming dissonance of life and death, of being and nonbeing, of having and losing that we confront. There can be no process of dealing with those dissonances of existence that does not hold ambiguity and dissonance in its own understanding.

Although we strive for a perceived sense of balance between loss and gain in the grief process, we need to keep in mind that it is only when we are off balance that we move forward. We cannot stand perfectly balanced, our weight distributed evenly between both legs, and then walk. We must shift our weight and take the risk of being unbalanced for a moment, and the dance is a series of successive moves that flow from balance to unbalance. We may not have chosen to become unbalanced, but we receive the opportunity to become familiar with that feeling and to learn to use it for growth and without fear.

Another way to understand the stages is to think of them as shifts of focus that grow in complexity within the spiral. So, in the Loss stage, we focus on the loved one; in the Return stage, we focus on ourselves; in the Reconnection stage, we focus on our relationship as including both the loved one and ourselves, and something more that grew out of our being together; and in the Creation stage, we focus on what was essential about our relationship with our loved one, and what new vision and creation emerges from that essence.

Some of us do well at letting go of our loved one but cling to our past selves; and some of us move on fine but never recognize the loss of the other. We need to both see the other as gone in the familiar terms *and* ourselves as being changed or different if we are to connect. And what connects is not the superficial of the past but the essential that transcends.

A relationship is comprised, of course, of 2 people. But a healthy relationship is more than just 2 people coming together in partnership for the purpose of fulfilling each other's needs, or even for the purpose of sharing the journey of life. A healthy relationship becomes an entity in itself – something more than the 2 partners that enhances both of them and has its own relationship to the family, community, and world in which it exists. So, the Reconnection stage is about discovering the essence of that relationship so that it can continue beyond the point when it ceases to be physical.

The process of Reconnection begins in the first stage, Loss, when and if we accept that our loved one is physically gone. As each calendar event is celebrated or marked without the physical presence of the loved one; as each piece of clothing or precious possession is given or put away, or becomes worn with use; as contact is made with each friend and family member who was physically connected to the lost loved one, and others die, move away, or just change and age; as homes are sold, children graduate or marry, cars are replaced; and as, little by little, the face of the world as we knew it with our loved one begins to look different, we begin the process of sorting out what was vital about our relationship.

So, Reconnection is essentially a sorting out process. We need to know what we can keep and what we cannot keep, and that is one reason it is so important to focus on reality rather than how we would like things to have been in the past or to be in the future. Focusing on what is not real for us, and/or what will never be real, diverts our energy from finding what persists and what we can incorporate into the future. We cannot make something a part of us and of our future relationship with our loved one if it does not and cannot exist. Will that future be filled with wishes and regrets, or will that future be filled with meaning and purpose? It's our choice.

Chapter 15
Resistance

As I have mentioned before, the process of Reconnection often starts in the Loss stage, and as you might have noticed, Reconnection and Loss are interwoven on the Grief Spiral. Sometimes, we become fixated on Reconnection and our physical separation from the loved one, and we are unable or unwilling to see our own identity as having changed. Although we feel that we have accepted the reality of the loss, and the "resolution" will appear as a sense of peace and resignation, our pain, while diminished in intensity, will remain of the same quality and tone. In other words, our experience of grief will become less overwhelming but our responses to thoughts and memories of the loved one will be exactly as they were in the beginning. Our fear of losing the past can keep us stuck in a loop, trying to reconnect to the loss while keeping our own identity static – or, more likely, denying the change in ourselves that has already occurred. Listening to the story of the loss, the perceptive companion or counselor will hear a calmer and more confident narrative, but the same plot and the same emotional responses to the events surrounding the loss.

Amy said, "What makes James real to me is my pain, not him as a separate person. Letting go of the pain would be letting go of him. I've accepted that James will be the pain till the day I die."

Here there is also the danger that we may become addicted to drugs or alcohol (or food or sex or attention or shopping, etc.) in an attempt to hold onto the past – even if it is at the expense of losing ourselves. We may use an addiction to freeze our own feelings as a way of preventing the perceived gap in time and space between us and our loved one from growing any wider or deeper. The fear of more loss is soothed by dependence on an external source of energy – even if that source leads to self-destruction. The external energy source not only provides comfort but also prevents addicts from creating their own energy for growth and progress. It is the protruding branch on the cliff that is clung to midway down as a griever falls; and to which she clings desperately even though it means an end to the journey, saps her energy as it is used to maintain the grip on a present that does not change, and precludes the possibility of receiving any help from others. Indeed, it is only when grievers – like addicts – let go and allow themselves to hit bottom that a way up can appear.

Moving from Loss to Reconnection is not the only

possible shortcut that some grievers might try to take. It is also possible to begin to move into the Return stage before we have dealt with all of the issues of the Loss stage and have come to accept the loss. As I said earlier, on the spiral of change the Loss stage is represented by the line that moves forward, and the Return stage by the line that curves backward into a loop but is really a continuation of forward motion. It is possible for grievers to stop short of Acceptance and become focused on the ways in which they themselves have changed. We may be so terrified of being separated from our loved one, and of feeling the pain of the psychological distance that comes with acceptance, that we may use the loved one's death as a catalyst for our own growth – as a way of recognizing and honoring the loved one and keeping him alive in our lives. We may idolize our loved one – or at least minimize his flaws – and use that distorted memory as an external energy source in a way similar to an addiction.

Eva had watched her 7-year-old son die 19 months earlier. She said, "I signed his body over. Brought his spirit home with me when I left the building he died in. I was never without him and still spend every day with him and we communicate. So I realize my son's not physically here. But who needs a body (dead weight). I mean I'm still who I am inside it. So I don't consider my son's life being over. I just consider he has evolved into another form. I will always miss the hugs and his cute little smile and that wink of his eye, meaning he loved me, without having to say the words. That will always cause me some form of pain. I will always cherish those things, it made me the richest person in the world. I accepted it before he died that I was going to lose him. I was lucky. Some moms don't get as long as I had with him – 7 wonderful years. His life is worthwhile, in so many ways. So is mine. We are both on the mission here daily and hope we can make the bridge for others to share. It pains us both as many hurt that way. I'm just like the messenger for him for all of mankind to share. He's trying to come back now and I'm trying to get pregnant."

At this point, as throughout the process, the need is to focus on reality. Part of that is recognizing the whole of the relationship – its positive *and* negative aspects.

The fear of separation may also manifest as rebellion – maintaining the connection with a loved one about whom we feel ambivalent by becoming as close to the opposite of him as possible. This gives us the illusion of separating, while in reality we are fused.

When Mark stopped drinking he began to realize that he had spent much of his energy trying to be what his dad had not been: an accepting and nonjudgmental father, a caring and compassionate friend, someone to whom emotions were of equal value to material success. He had tried to hold his family together at any cost because he remembered how painful his own parents' divorce had been to him. He said, "I used to say, 'I'll never be like him.' But when I got into recovery I had to admit I was."

I think it is important here to remember what I said before: that it is the *momentum* that is the key to navigating the grief process. As long as we are moving, we are moving in the right direction. So, while the seeming shortcuts noted above might look like mistakes, they are simply ways of dealing with the fear and pain that are always present to some extent on the journey. A griever who takes one of the shortcuts will find their way as long as they keep moving. The only real problem we need be mindful of is getting stuck and choosing to stop the momentum in order to avoid some consequence that the griever fears – the permanent loss of the loved one, an empty future, a changed identity that changes the past, etc. So while the shortcuts and detours are often normal parts of the Grief Spiral, it can be helpful to address those types of fears before they become obstacles that can stop the griever. Once the momentum has stopped, it can be hard to get going again because the energy required to do so might not be available.

Since resistant grievers have not achieved the level of peace that is the hallmark of the resolution of the Loss stage, they can often be distinguished by their agitated, hyper, inappropriately and excessively cheerful, compulsive, distracted, or driven demeanor – appearing almost to be controlled by forces outside themselves. It is critical for counselors to help them revisit the past and revisit the phases of the process that were bypassed.

Griever's Toolbox:

If dealing with the first type of resistance:
* ★ Keep your focus on all the ways in which you have changed, and explore the significance of your pain.
* ★ Engage in enjoyable and energizing activities.
* ★ Be aware of any incipient addictions.

If dealing with the second type of resistance:
* ★ Remember and write about your loved one's flaws, the conflicts between you, and the ways in which you were similar.
* ★ Do the Positive... Negative exercise (Appendix A).
* ★ Focus on your own strengths.
* ★ Engage in enjoyable and energizing activities.

Counseling Interventions:

If dealing with the first type of resistance:

★ Educate the griever about the purpose addictions serve.

If dealing with the second type of resistance:

★ Keep bringing the griever back to the elements of the Loss stage and explore his fears to determine where the stuck point is.

Chapter 16
Recognition

When we accept our loss *and* move into the Return stage, we deal with how we have changed; and as we do that, we often realize that our changing has changed the relationship.

Emily said, "Connecting to my own loving and peaceful place is where I connect most deeply to Megan's spirit, and I truly never let her go. I am only learning a new way to be with her. But I must let go of the old and be in that horrible empty place before she can come in her new form to me."

In the Reconnection stage, we begin to recognize that not only are the roles we played in relation to our loved one gone; the roles our loved one played in relation to *us* are gone, too. Here we see that not only are we no longer children, parents, partners, spouses, grandchildren, siblings, or friends; but our loved one is no longer our parent, child, partner, spouse, grandparent, sibling, or friend. The identity of our loved one is not essentially embedded in the roles she played, but in who she was.

Similarly, she is no longer African American, Latino, Asian, Catholic, Jewish, Hindu, Italian, Russian, rich, homeless, ill, successful, handicapped, well-groomed, athletic, overweight, bald, young, blue-eyed, or tall. Our task at this step is to discover the essential identity of our loved one – *who* she was apart from *what* she was – and find a way to reconnect, so that the relationship can continue without holding either us or the loved one back, in memory or reality.

If you are grieving the loss of a beloved husband who was an overweight 27-year-old Hindu athlete (yes, I know that sounds a little absurd!), ponder how you would recognize him if he came home one day in the guise of a slim 47-year-old Catholic college professor. What qualities or ways of being would give his identity away to those who know him intimately? What was unmistakably *him* to you? Is there a symbol or image you can think of that would represent the essence of his identity?

Amy met a Native American man at work and asked him how Native Americans mourn the death of an infant. He told her a story about James's spirit being with other children's spirits. He said the Creator was telling them stories and they were laughing and making fun of Him behind His back. The man said, "Let him go. He's in a better place than we are. He's free." Amy said, "I cried happy tears, and I saw an image of James as a butterfly as he talked. Afterwards I felt like a ton had been lifted off my shoulders. I never thought of him that way before. That was the first time I felt warm in my heart for James. I was so grateful to that man I wanted him to feel warm, too, so I bought him a pair of warm socks."

Emily said, "Megan loved rocks her whole life! When she died, she had an extensive rock collection . . . makes me smile to think of it. Where most people keep jewelry in their jewelry boxes, she also had rocks. And in her drawers under lacy under things, more rocks! So when that little butterfly settled on a rock, I knew once again our Megan was enjoying what she loved most, nature and her beloved rocks! O how I cannot wait for that day when I too am with her and can understand how incredibly freeing and spectacular our next life, our real life, really is! I love you, my butterfly child! When I am able to be free of my pain for a time, I can only feel the most incredible joy that you are now safe and free in a way I cannot even imagine!"

Griever's Toolbox:

★ Name all the roles your loved one played and all the elements of her physical identity.

★ Name a symbol (or symbols) that describe the essence of your loved one's identity.

Counseling Interventions:

★ Educate the griever about the necessity to distinguish between *what* the loved one was and *who* the loved one was. Explore any confusion of that differentiation.

Chapter 17
Separation

The process we undertake of sorting out the many facets of our loved one's life and his relationship to our lives is really a process of separation. It is only by focusing – alternately or simultaneously – on what the loved one no longer is physically, and on what we can keep from the relationship and take with us into the world of our future, that we can separate without feeling we have lost all of who the loved one was. To try to separate without knowing, or at least hoping, that not everything will be lost is to fail. We will simply not go there, or we will find a way to sabotage the process. And to try to forget selectively that which we find too painful to remember is to risk forgetting other things that we will need to remember in order to reconnect.

Many people just try to forget, feeling that forgetting is easier than the pain of separation. Separation is something that can feel final and frightening, especially when our loved one is no longer physical and already is separate from us in that way. We don't want to let any more of our loved one go. So, separation must be approached mindfully, consciously, and patiently, and with the emphasis on the eventual reunion so that hope is sustained.

At this step, we are trying to unlearn the physical relationship we had so that we can move forward into a new way of relationship. We can only unlearn by replacement. No gaps, just a new building block, because what we had learned is embedded in a web of being. Take out a piece, and *plop*. But change a piece, and a whole web changes with it. A mundane example: If we decide to quit eating meat, we will die if all we are eating is the other stuff we had with the meat. But put the replacement in place first, then we can more easily unlearn. This is one reason that AA (Alcoholics Anonymous) is so effective. The alcoholic is not just asked to give up drinking, but given a new way to relate that adds to and expands his web of being.

Losing and forgetting is not the same as changing one's perspective. So, this step is not as much about the need to *let go* as most of us understand that term, as it is about the need to suspend holding on. As long as we remain stuck like super glue to the physical image of who our loved one was, we will not be able to reconnect with who she is and what that means to us. When we are willing to let the past be in the past – where we can visit it from time to time but not live in it – we can close the door of the past just enough to allow the door to the future to open.

Joshua, a Unitarian Universalist minister, told a story that illustrates the difficulty of Reconnection when feelings are ambivalent, and the rewards when it is achieved: "I did my father's memorial service. I pointed out all the positive aspects of his existence, did not mention the problems in our relationship. I held out throughout the service, and after the 'final' amen, broke down crying, owning my loss.

"My father had disapproved of my vocation as a minister. He would have wanted me to be a successful businessman, as he had been, and business was not my cup of tea, hence would lead to failure. However ministry too had great challenges; and without the paternal blessing, I struggled along. I was a rebel with a cause, many causes: civil rights, police brutality, Vietnam War, counseling, New Age, and clashed with many parishioners of different persuasions. My father would have been on the side of the antagonists. He was prejudiced, an anti-Communist crusader, opposed to counseling, considered the little he knew of New Age as hocus-pocus. I was caught between filial respect and disagreements on issues. How does one grieve the loss of a parent with whom one is at odds?

"At a Unitarian Universalist summer camp, I asked a medium to give me a message from my dad. That was *about 2 years after dad's passing. She said what I wanted to hear: My father now understood, and approved of my vocation. It was a great relief, his acceptance of me, and meanwhile I turned around and started to relate to some of his life's wisdom. I quote him often in my mind, or in conversation with my spouse. I am grateful that he was part of bringing me into life. I gradually felt more and more reconciled and was able to reconnect. With the benefit of hindsight, this liberated me for a new creation. My ministry started to go deeper and I became more attuned to my parishioners, more loving, more respected by them. Not having to fight my dad, I did not have to fight my parishioners anymore."*

This phase requires a great deal of patience, for often those aspects of our relationship with our loved one that we must leave behind and those we can incorporate into who we are and are becoming are not immediately evident or clear. It sometimes takes experimentation to discover what we do need or want to incorporate as opposed to what we think we *should* incorporate. Some grievers think that they should focus on the circumstances of their loved one's death and take that on as their own by joining a cause or advocating research into trying to prevent that type of harm from coming to others. They become Mothers Against Drunk Driving or activists for cancer research, and in that way feel they are expressing an aspect of their loved one in a way that heals others. But if that aspect is not also their own – if that focus is not fulfilling for them – then, not only will they risk getting stuck in focusing on the event of the death, but they will not really find reconnection.

Separation involves a process of distinguishing between what our loved one valued and what we value; between what our loved one needed from our relationship and what we needed; between what our loved one learned from his experiences and what we learned and remembered. Although we shared relationship with our loved one, we are not the same as our loved one, and our learnings will not be meaningful to us in the same way they were to him. So an aspect of the Separation phase is incorporating the loved one into our life in our own way, not in the loved one's way. Otherwise we will reconnect neither with him as he was, nor with ourselves as they are becoming, but with some chimera of the past that never existed and so is incapable of moving us toward fulfillment.

Selene told me, "At around 8 or 9 months after my mom-in-law's passing all I could remember was feeling bad that I had gotten busy. Me doing things I had never done, going out, socializing more often and pursuing my spirituality. *I actually felt bad that I was living my life, as opposed to caring for her. I say spirituality because during her illness, which was bone cancer, I learned something called Reiki. It's an old Japanese method of relaxation and healing on the levels of physical, mental, emotional, spiritual. I learned it because I was desperate to heal her, to save her, to keep her with me. So here I am now in this place of having dealt with her passing and having a sense of purpose in learning more about the Reiki which did not save her life, but she did feel comfort and her pain was lessened.*

"*I began feeling that perhaps I honored her best by doing what I loved, which is to teach Reiki. She encouraged me, she inspired me when she was here and I got to thinking that there must have been a reason within this sadness that we both explored Reiki together–me as the channel and her as a willing receiver. I found her in many ways during this time period in my life – in my Reiki, in my raising of my children. It's as though I would hear her voice in my head with advice as to how to soothe them or console them when they cried for her. I was learning to let go and to let her be a part of my life in a different way. We began to put her picture on the table during holiday dinners, we hung butterflies and said "Hi gramma" when one flew by us. We smiled again and felt joyful at the synchronicities that occurred and made us aware of her. We embraced this new love, and it felt like a new love of her. A conscious awareness of her and us being connected in a positive way. Each of us was different because of her passing. My family learned to treasure each day and each moment of love because of our experience. My husband focused on his family instead of work, my kids focused on compassion for their grandpa and others, and I focused on finding out why we can feel so close to loved ones who have passed without actually 'seeing' them."*

It also takes experimentation to sort out what was vital and valuable in memory but can be relegated to the past. Thinking in terms of a big sheet of paper divided into 3 columns: Past, Present, and Future, and putting each aspect of the loved one and our relationship with him in one of the columns, can be very helpful – whether or not the list is actually made on a real piece of paper. Grievers often get confused between the past, present, and future, and we tend to think of ourselves as we were in the past even though we understand intellectually that we have changed. Looking back and remembering in detail how we were in the past, how we responded, what we thought, what we enjoyed, what our priorities were, and where we focused our energies; repeating that process in terms of the present; and repeating that process again in terms of the loved one, and then again in terms of the relationship with our loved one can give us clarity and direction and insight into how we can move our relationship into the future.

Griever's Toolbox:

★ Make a chart with 3 columns entitled "Past," "Present," and "Future." List all the attributes of your loved one and sort out who she was, what aspects of the relationship are still parts of your world, and what you can or want to take into the future. Include the following:

- How you were in the past (more materialistic, controlling, individualistic, protective, etc., what you learned, how you will take that into the future)

- Physical roles: How your loved one was (s/he loved movies, you could start or expand on a collection and watch them with others; s/he loved animals, you could get a pet or volunteer at an animal shelter)

- Essential roles (s/he was more social than you, you could expand your social network and have more dinner parties; s/he was a better listener, you could take a course in communication skills and then practice that with others, etc.)

- Essential characteristics (loving, courageous, creative, honest, etc.)

★ Focus on sorting out, rather than letting go.

★ Be patient. This phase often resurfaces at many points in the process.

★ If you have kept a journal in the past, or have letters you wrote or videos of yourself, go back to them.

★ Begin journaling now if you are not already doing it or have stopped doing it.

★ Think about your priorities, how they have changed, and how they are similar to or different from the loved one's priorities. Go through the same process with favorite activities, places, clothing, attitudes, hobbies, food, movies, books, music, spiritual paths, politics, or whatever else comes to mind.

Counseling Interventions:

★ Be alert for other ways to bring the "Past-Present-Future" theme into therapy sessions. If the griever has a skill or talent, think together about how to express the theme using that talent (through poetry, art, music, gardening, acting, carpentry, etc.).

★ Facilitate the client's sorting-out process in relation to whatever topic comes up. Keep the focus on how they have changed, and how different from and/or similar they are to the loved one.

Chapter 18
Rejoining

When we have separated, we become aware of what we have lost, what needs to be let go, and what we always had and therefore could never have lost. Like Dorothy in *The Wizard of Oz*, we understand that we have always had the power to go back to Kansas, but first needed to learn for ourselves that if our heart's desire is not in our own backyard, we never really lost it to begin with. We come to understand that the relationship we treasured with our loved one was only physically embodied in her; spiritually and psychologically it was, and is, just as vitally within us.

This is essentially a spiritual process, because it involves every aspect of who we are, of who our loved one was, and of our relationship. The rejoining is always a spiritual rejoining, but it may or may not take the form of a psychic rejoining. It can involve spiritual paths such as meditation, channeling, dream work, etc. But even if it does not, it is still a spiritual process that connects us to something larger than our self. A healthy relationship always creates something more than the two people involved. It becomes an entity in itself, in which the couple participates, to which the couple give their energies, and from which they derive sustenance and happiness. That larger entity also enhances its social context. So, when one of the participants in the relationship dies, part of who they were and what they contributed to the larger entity remains. The relationship changes form, but is never lost.

At this step, we are ready to rejoin with our loved one in a way that honors her, ourselves, and the relationship – fondly remembering all those things that were uniquely part of who she was, keeping alive the things of substance she was about, and sharing the dreams of the future she had.

Leonardo, 53, whose wife died, said, "One day I realized a number of ways in which I had taken on some of her character traits and interests. My love for flowers blossomed, my knowledge of homeopathy (an alternative healing modality that she was proficient in) deepened, I was becoming a better hands-on healer (it was Esperanza who originally got me interested in becoming a healer). And at times I would find myself seeing things or thinking about things the way she used to. I know that those kinds of things happen a lot when people are married, but I felt them deepen after Esperanza's passing.

"As time went on, I became uncomfortable referring to her as my late wife. Even though those are the best

words to use when describing her to others, I began to realize that thinking about her that way was keeping me in the past. I have a relationship with her now. But I didn't know how to describe this relationship, so I started calling her a guardian angel, a very special guardian angel who I know very well."

Here is where we begin in earnest the task of embodying our loved one's presence in our being, in our actions, and in the world. Part of this process may be trying on various behaviors that we had previously identified with her, but not with ourselves. For example, if our loved one was more social than we were, we might try doing more entertaining or partying – thus joining our experience with hers. This may or may not prove to be something we feel like practicing as a pattern of behavior indefinitely, but it will provide a sense of closeness and continuity of relationship. We may wish to reconnect with our loved one's friends – understanding that they will probably perceive us as being, or representing, her in those relationships. These ways of behaving can not only help us to express what we have learned about the loved one, and to teach ourselves that the relationship abides within us; but it can assuage feelings of guilt and propel another small step toward letting go.

Jessica had had a friend, Lisa, since elementary school and Martha had become close to her as well, treating her like part of their family. Martha decided to call Lisa, whom she had not seen in years. She dreaded doing it because of the memories it would recall, but as soon as Lisa realized who was calling and Martha heard the joy and tears in her voice, the dread evaporated. They agreed to meet at a restaurant, and Martha said, "It was just like we did this all the time. We still love each other and feel like we're each a part of Jessica. Hugging her was the best part! And, you know it's funny, but sometimes when I was talking to Lisa it was almost like Jessica's words were coming out of my mouth. That felt comforting."

Grievers will often say that they know their loved one better since her death than they did when she was alive. It is a psychological truism that, when we are emotionally involved with someone, we can rarely perceive them – or ourselves as we are in that relationship – without our own needs and expectations distorting the image. When someone dies, those needs and expectations cannot be fulfilled, and they start to fade into the background, as a truer and clearer image of the one gone emerges into the foreground. Grievers also tend to pay more attention when others talk about how they knew and related to the loved one, and that adds dimension to their own perceptions. Consequently, they may say things like, "I wish I knew then what I know now. I would have been or done better, or differently."

Martha was about to leave on a trip to Mexico – a place Jessica always wanted to go. "I'm still not sure I want to go," she said, "but I'm packing some of her things to take with me and wear there. I've learned my own strength, and I've learned some things that Jessica knew: life is short and there are no guarantees, enjoy it and don't focus so much on work, take that 'extra minute' for others, you can't control everything . . . my priorities have changed. I wish I was more like I am now with Jessica, but I know I couldn't be before while I was trying to make a future for her. I'm letting go."

"It's ok," George said, "I don't seem to be getting as upset or down as I was before. I've more accepted it than I have in the past. I'm thinking more about the future and I'm not as afraid of it as I was . . . I'm smarter than I thought I was. I used to think about what it would be like if my parents died. I thought I'd be devastated, crushed. I didn't think I'd be as strong as I am." He was incorporating aspects of his parents into himself (by learning to cook, handling their financial matters in a

competent manner, taking their role in relation to his aunts, etc.) and discovering his own identity. He told me about 2 dreams he had – one about his mom and one about his dad – in which he was helping them. Their roles had reversed. He was seeing himself as his own parents. When they were alive and ill he had taken on a caretaking role but still perceived himself as "the son" emotionally. Now that had changed. "I feel like I have done a lot of growing," George said. "When I talk to older people I'm more talkative. I feel more like their equal and less like a child. I feel better as a person."

Revisiting places of the past can be therapeutic at this step. By doing this we can accomplish 3 things:
1. We can reclaim parts of the past that had been lost, or distorted in memory, with the loss of the loved one, and regain a sense of continuity with the present.
2. We can experience how we have changed in a setting where we and the loved one had a physical relationship.
3. We can have a new experience there, and so we can bring the place of the past with us into the future.

This revisiting might entail going back to an earlier home or neighborhood, a school, or even a favorite vacation spot. At this step we are allowing ourselves to be changed by the death of our loved one. As we experience that changed self – which is the re-union of the relationship – in an environment that will seem at once familiar and strange, we will be able to go forward without it and the past will feel less present.

Chloe had been thinking about returning to Japan to reconnect with that part of her heritage and the language she had lost in childhood. She wanted to take a course in Japanese first. She felt conflicted culturally, as though a "tug of war is going on between the American and Japanese parts of me. I need to reconcile the two and mesh it into me and what I think and feel and believe."

George talked about the healing effects of being in his childhood home. "I can feel the past there, and I can see what I've learned from them and how I'm becoming more and more like them. Like my mom, I can handle complicated financial transactions and I didn't know that before. I'm more concerned with my appearance, the way she was. I'm proud of how much better I look now and reward myself with small gifts like she would give me. And I'm more like my dad in the way I relate to people – especially to children. I'm easier to talk to, more open, less self-conscious. I've become a pretty good cook. And I can also see that I don't avoid dealing with my feelings the way he did. I think that being in their house has made things clearer to me. I'm grateful for my mom's love, and for the relationship I had with my parents. Now I'm looking toward selling their house and it feels a little overwhelming, thinking about letting that last thing go. But I'll leave something of myself there – bury something in the backyard. It will be a new start. I want to go forward and keep growing. And I know my mom is still there looking out for me."

Here is my favorite definition of grief: *Grief is the recognition that we have to surrender to the past something we wish was in the present and future.* But we still have it if we put it in perspective. In fact, if we do not put it in perspective, we do not have it; it has us and we are stopped on our own journey. But if we rejoin our loved one in a way that expresses the essence of who we are, who the loved one is, and what the relationship is about, we will discover that we are moving toward making meaning of our loss. Connection is spirit to spirit, not person to person. So Reconnection is the stage in which 2 spirits deprived of their physical connections reconnect.

Sandy Goodman (author of Love Never Dies, a book about her spiritual grief journey after her son's death) shared the following with me:
"I think we know we've made it to the Reconnection

stage when we get honest with ourselves. I remember one particular conversation with Jason while sitting on the still damp grass at the cemetery.

"'Jason,' I had said, 'I would give anything to have you back . . . anything at all.' It was a standard line, one I had repeated over and over, both silently and aloud, for nearly four years. I had become fairly comfortable saying I had found gifts in Jason's dying, but would assuage my guilt by following the statement with '. . . but I would give them all up in a minute to have my son back.'

"This time though, I felt pushed to analyze what I was actually saying. Did I want my life to be as it was before? Did I yearn for the old me whose priority in life was deciding where to go for dinner on Saturday night? Did I miss yelling at Jason for leaving his dishes in the living room and his socks in the kitchen? Would I be happy with the old me and the old Jason knowing what I know now? Something wasn't clicking.

"When I said, 'I would give anything to . . .' I wanted the physical manifestation of the Jason now living in spirit. What I wanted, and would have given anything for, was the physical connection of the spirit of me and the spirit of Jason. Once again, I had let my ego's want for the tangible to overpower my heart's need for the love . . .

"Smiling, I closed my eyes and called Jason into the

picture once more. 'Hey. Cancel that last statement. I know. I already have you "back." You never really left . . ."

The response of many of us at this point in the process is often, "Oh!" as we then are able to hear the answer within to all those *why* questions we asked at the beginning of our grief process. We hear the questions answered in the reflections and echoes of all we have experienced since then. Listen to the voices of those going through this phase and you will hear pride, wistfulness, excitement about the future, and more looking forward than looking back.

Griever's Toolbox:

★ View the film *The Wizard of Oz*. Write about the theme of grieving the loss or lack of something external that is actually internal.

★ Choose one aspect of the loved one's life, relationships, abilities, or personality that you want to embody and keep alive in the physical world. Think of this as a healing activity or experiment, not an assignment.

★ Connect with friends or relatives of the loved one – representing the loved one to them, and sharing stories and memories.

★ Write about what you have learned about your loved one that you did not know before the death.

★ Wear a linking object, such as a locket containing the loved one's photo or an item of the loved one's clothing.

★ Since this phase is part of identity formation, it can be helpful to keep a dream journal. Dreams often offer options or directions and may open up possibilities you are not consciously aware of (see Appendix A).

★ Revisit places you had been with your loved one.

Counseling Interventions:

★ Encourage the griever to keep a dream journal, and assist with dream interpretation.

★ Focus on how much the griever has learned up to this point. Keep repeating the changes you see in her, and asking her to tell you about how she has changed and grown through the grief process so far.

Chapter 19
Balance

When we find balance, we can stop grieving because then we will lose no more. We keep grieving until we can do that. The balance is between the reality of the past and the reality of the future – between what was lost and what has been gained. And we will lose no more because we have reconnected with our loved one's essential self and let go of what was solely physical. Just as we cannot walk or dance without tipping over unless we have first arrived at a balance on both feet, we cannot move on from grief unless we have first arrived at a psychic balance between what we have lost and what we have gained. Just as we who carry something heavy need to hold it close in order to balance, we need to hold our grief close to us while its weight is immediate and compelling. But as we proceed through the grief process, the weight of the grief decreases and we can move in alignment with grace and equilibrium.

When we are standing on one foot, it's hard to move forward. So, too, when we are focusing on one dimension of our experience – the past. But when we find balance, moving forward becomes possible.

Another metaphor I have found helpful is that of the river, with one shore representing the past and the other representing the future. When we leave the past shore and swim toward the future, we will find the pull backwards stronger than the hope of reaching the other shore until we are past the midpoint. It is when we begin to achieve a balance between the pain of loss and the joy of discovery that we have moved forward from midstream and are closer to the far shore of the river. I say, "begin to achieve," because this is a process, not an event.

One indication that we have reached Balance is that we will talk more about the future. The past will seem less compelling. The future will seem more exciting than scary, and we will express less resistance to trying new things or new behaviors. The counselor will also hear that revisiting the thoughts, feelings, and experiences of the past no longer yields anything productive, revelatory, or more than factual, and that clients will respond with greater energy when the conversation shifts to what they have learned from their grief journey and what lies ahead.

Amy showed me a beautiful heart-shaped découpage memory box she had made. It was purple and covered in photographs she had taken of clouds. In it was a letter tied with a ribbon that she had written to parents of stillborns or infants who died in the hospital with suggestions on how to cope and heal, a pewter locket, and a candle. She said, "I want to make a lot of these boxes and donate them to hospitals and doctors so that they can give them to parents to make the baby a person. I wouldn't have known they needed that before it happened to me. If I can just help one person it will make everything I've been through worthwhile."

When we have found balance, we can reach out to others and share what we have learned. In fact, part of moving into new patterns is realizing how what we have learned can help others who are on the grief journey. As we do that, we realize how far we've come.

Thinking again in energy terms, it is not until some portion of an energy field changes that it can creatively emerge in newness. When we resist filling with newness the spaces left by a change – by any change in direction or behavior – we risk remaining static or off balance and being consumed by the past, because there are no voids we can tolerate for long and we will fall back into old patterns. What we hold onto in fear keeps us the same – which we like because it feels familiar – but it also keeps us from growth. And the bound foot of the ancient Chinese courtesan may have been appealing, but it was also excruciatingly painful.

So the task of the next stage is Creation.

Griever's Toolbox:

★ Use this metaphor: You are swimming across a river and, until you are halfway across, you will feel the pull backwards stronger than the desire to reach the far shore (which still looks uncertain and covered with fog). When you reach the midpoint and begin to look forward as much as backward, you will have achieved balance. Ponder where you are in that river.

★ Reach out to others who are behind you on their grief journey. Sometimes by helping others we begin to see how far we have come, and that keeps us moving toward a new future.

Counseling Interventions:

★ Provide support and encouragement, and prepare the griever for the next phase of the process.

Stage 4: Creation

Why do you stay in prison
when the door is so wide open?

Move outside the tangle of fear-thinking.
Live in silence.

Flow down and down in always
widening rings of being.

- Rumi (from *A Community of the Spirit*)

Chapter 20
Creation

Creation. This is *Genesis*: the emergence of a new reality that takes shape as we focus on what is possible and are able to act on our vision of what is already-but-not-yet. Recovery is not about having all as it was before, nor is it about fixing or compensation; recovery is about living, enjoying, and finding meaning in our changed world. All that we have learned from our loved one, ourselves, and our relationship has changed our field of experience; and the next step is living in that new field of raw materials, accessing it, interacting with it, and thus realizing it – as in, making it real. In the diagram of the spiral, this stage is the line that continues forward and outward from the intersection.

As we move through the Grief Spiral, each phase can be understood as a shift in focus. In Loss, we focus on our loved one; in Return, on ourself; in Reconnection, on our relationship; and in Creation, on the future that includes all of that and more.

Here new things come from the connection. In most life connections, we do not want others to change, and even fear it. We connect to people over time to get what we expect; our perception of them fits that which we feel we need or want. If they begin to change, we feel threatened and/or confused, as though we had been betrayed or a promise had been broken. We may become angry and try everything we can think of to pull the other person back into the relationship pattern as it was. But in this reconnection we welcome the creative changes because we know they do not change the essence, only the product. It is through the creative changes that we are able to express our loved one's ongoing presence in our lives. It's what keeps our loved one as a living, as opposed to static, presence. What we discovered in Reconnection needs to be put into practice. We can reconnect to the essence – the seed of who our loved one was. But unless we choose to actively plant and nurture that seed in the new soil of our future, it becomes a static artifact of our relationship, and loses its aliveness.

Healthy relationships are those that focus on the creation of something greater than self, rather than on meeting the individual needs of their participants. They build on each other's strengths, rather than trying to compensate for each other's weaknesses. Two people who are whole join in relationship to create a family so they can connect to others through their love and make their world a better place; a group of business associates join together to create a company that will produce something to enhance the way people live; an artist joins his talent with the resources of a gallery to create a connection that will inspire the public, and so on. And in the process of this type of creation, individuals find fulfillment, because what they create is a positive expression of their being.

Unhealthy relationships are those that focus on meeting the needs of their individual members, maintaining stability at any cost, and resisting change. This is the dilemma faced by families of addicts or alcoholics. In order to sustain itself, the family system evolves and revolves around its most dysfunctional member. It is a method of compensation rather than enhancement. The compensation by some members of the system for the lack of active energy exchange by another member makes the system dysfunctional and throws it off balance. While this can work in the short run, in the long run it serves neither the system nor any of its members. The dysfunctional member's destructive and self-destructive behavior is sustained, and the effort expended by other members of the system drains their own energy resources for growth and fulfillment. They often will subsequently form relationships that are also dysfunctional in an effort to rebalance the system – similar to the dynamic involved when a widower remarries quickly because he cannot balance on his own – but the focus on remedies is a focus on the past, and cannot lead to a healthier future.

Grievers are people who had a connection with someone they loved for what they expected or wanted or needed from that person. Now that person is gone. So, they are left with 3 choices:

1. Try to continue to relate to the loved one as she was.
2. Try to "get over it" and move on in the loved one's absence as though she were never there.
3. Deal with the changed relationship and allow for new things and ways of being and relating to evolve from it.

The first 2 are ways of compensation, and will lead to dysfunction. The third is a way of enhancement that can lead toward fulfillment. And the way to it is the way through the fear of change – the fear that pulls our focus back to control, guilt, anger, and depression.

After a loss we need to let go. It is only by losing our life that we find it. It is only by leaving Circle #1 that we live in Circle #2. In other words, it is only by losing our old life that we find our new one. Easy to say, extremely difficult to do. This is why grievers need so much support. Not because they are weak and need to adjust so they can resume living their life as it was before the loss, but because they need to learn a new (and usually better) way of being and of living.

At the Creation stage, grievers who have reached

Balance learn to focus more on what is in the glass than on whether it is half empty or half full – both of which perspectives imply a lack. The pain of scarcity becomes the recognition of abundance, and the agony of remaining static becomes the joy of growth. For to remain static is to deny the opportunities that any change presents, and that kind of grief never is resolved and never is even fully accepted. When we begin to focus on abundance is when we begin to see the opportunities for creativity – what was earlier perceived as a vast, empty abyss is now seen as containing the raw materials out of which new life can spring. The fear of change dissipates, and although it remains uncomfortable it is accepted as the stuff of life – that which transforms potential into reality.

Chapter 21
Change

Most people resist natural change. Many of us stop at some point – or more typically at multiple points – in the process and say something like, "I can't take anymore." But in crossing a river it does no good to stop in the middle. The great fear is really that the situation will not change *enough* – that the absence of our loved one will be the only change we experience – and that fear keeps us from being open to enough change. Those who suffer change are those who do not let it play out, and the red flag that lets us know that there is more to come that will bring us into balance is when the pain of loss is greater than the reward of change.

Having recognized that she needed to express her artistic and creative abilities, Chloe said, "I feel I'm holding back. I'm afraid of rejection. But I feel like I'm missing something. I know I need to take the risk, but I'm a perfectionist. What if I fail? I know it comes from my childhood. The message was, 'If you're less than perfect, you don't exist.'" I asked her what the advantages were of not doing anything about it. "I don't have to face my fears," she replied, "I'm always wondering and don't have to take the risk. The disadvantage is I'll never know till I put myself out there."

In order to be able to create, we must be able to accept change as the fundamental process of all life. Why? Because *creation* means the discovery of newness. And in order to be able to accept change, we need to learn how to live with uncertainty, ambiguity, paradox, and confusion. We all find it easy to accept that which we want, but if we only accepted what we wanted we would only get a little of what we could – and nothing new. It takes the risk of opening to the painful and the trivial and the unknown to also get the serendipitous and the spiritual and the redemptive. It takes the ability to see seeming contradictions as parts of the same whole to get the discovery of new and creative connections. So one of the tasks of this step is to become accustomed to a wider horizon that we are not yet able to see clearly in detail; to be open to the inherent possibilities of life rather than trying to anticipate what will happen; to trust that there will be *something* – even though we cannot know precisely what it is – and that it will be meaningful.

George said he saw the future in general terms, but

did not have specific goals. "I expect that things will happen for a reason," he mused.

Some grievers seem to intuitively understand the need to be open to discovery and change quite early on in the process, others take a longer time, and others resist out of fear. I have found it helpful for fearful clients when I point out the ways in which they have already changed and remind them of how scary where they are now seemed at that earlier point in the process. This instills hope, and the courage to move forward and take another small step. It is also worth mentioning here that just because a concept is understood intellectually, or even intuitively, does not mean a griever will be capable of translating that understanding into action – especially when there is no professional support.

Another metaphor I use is that of a circle, representing a person's energy field, with smaller circles within it. At the beginning of the process much energy goes into dealing with issues from the past (I draw *P*s inside the smaller circles), and as those issues get resolved energy is released and the *P*s become *?*s, which represent unknown or future behavior patterns. It feels scary and confusing, and many grievers revert to their old "P" patterns for comfort. In fact, almost everyone does that in stressful situations. Often that need for the comfort of the familiar –

the need *not* to have to expend limited energy on creating or maintaining new patterns – is perceived as regression, but it usually lasts only until the griever has enough energy to move forward again.

Chloe said, "I know now that perfection is not possible. I want to get out of my comfort zone." I said, "You already are! Remember, there's no way to feel 'ready' for something new, because what it is is unknown." Chloe replied, "I need to choose one new thing to try."

After reconnecting with the loved one – or during Reconnection – grievers can move toward reconnecting with life. Recovery from loss is about reestablishing a 1:1 ratio with life rather than looking at life as an antagonist, or at we ourselves as victims. When we lose someone physically, we also lose the relationship we had with life itself. But life did not leave us, we left it, and we need to find our way back. And the way back is through integrating ourselves into a larger perspective that includes not only what we want and expect but also what life has offered us, which is always and inevitably change.

Miriam, whose daughter Rachel had died 5 years

earlier, used to spend hours each day on the Internet. She would search out all of the chat room mediumship readings to feel connected with her daughter. "Now," Miriam said, "change is what I am seeking in my life. We have sold our house, and are moving to a smaller house. I am seeking new people, new thoughts. The 'same old' just isn't getting it anymore. I talk to Rachel myself, and, yes, I still enjoy a reading from time to time, but to sit in a chat room hour after hour hoping to get a small message is just not me anymore." Her spiritual search led Miriam to establish a wellness center, which offers many classes and services to her community.

A kind of accord treaty with life is adopted. When we can come to terms with change, we come to terms with life and are open to receiving what it has to offer in return for the loss, and that hackneyed phrase "God never gives us more than we can handle" may take on new meaning as we cease to interpret it in terms of what happened to us, and begin to see that the choices we have made to *deal with* what happened to us have led us to a place we would not have chosen to go. Our war with life ends. There is no victory, no defeat, no battle at all; there is instead the recognition that much has been gained in the aftermath of what once felt like the ultimate defeat, and that in itself can shift our perspective from focusing on loss to focusing on possibility. It is with that acquiescence to life that peace emerges along with trust in the process.

Martha talked about future possibilities, considering ways in which she could share what she'd learned with others. She said, "I love working with kids. Maybe I'll do some tutoring. They have a program at work where I can help elementary school kids. I'm going to take the hospice volunteer training. I want to talk to people who are dying or grieving, and I think I'd be good at that because of what I've learned and remembered from talking to you." She was looking forward to taking a trip next year to Spain. She also expressed a strong desire to continue her spiritual search and develop her psychic abilities. During that session, for the very first time, Martha was able to say, "Jessica died."

So, the first step in Creation is coming to terms with change, because if nothing is perceived as new then nothing new will be created. And if nothing is perceived as new then anything experienced as meaningful will be about repetition or replication, not creation.

Griever's Toolbox:

★ Use the image of the 2 intersecting circles. You have found what persists in both circles (the area of intersection), and now need to discover what is waiting in Circle #2.

★ Focus on your strengths, talents, and abilities.

★ Engage in spiritual and/or religious exploration. Think about what you need from a spiritual perspective. Consider various forms of spiritual practice (see Appendix A).

★ Try new things, and make a hobby or game out of finding new people, places, and experiences (e.g., never going to the same restaurant twice, going somewhere new on vacation, seeking out a new friend, etc.).

★ View the film *It's a Wonderful Life*. Write about the losses and changes that the main character experiences.

★ Continue to keep a Gratitude Journal.

★ Write your own obituary. How do you want to be remembered?

Counseling Interventions:

★ Frequently affirm how far the griever has come and how much she has gained through the grief process in spite of her fears.

★ Assist the griever in moving forward on a spiritual path.

★ Use this metaphor: Draw a circle, representing the griever's energy field, with smaller circles within it. Draw *P*s inside the smaller circles to represent issues from the past, and explain that as those issues get resolved energy is released and the *P*s become *?*s, which represent unknown or future behavior patterns. The unknown can feel scary and confusing, and many of us revert to our old *P* patterns for comfort. Those *?*s now need to become new experiences. If they do not, then the griever will get stuck trying to make past patterns meaningful in a future where they do not fit. This is a good metaphor to use whenever you feel the griever is resisting or fearing change.

★ If the griever protests that she wants to change something but is not ready, remind her that we can never be ready for a change because we do not know what it will be like until we get there. Talk about previous changes that did not turn out exactly the way the griever expected.

Chapter 22
Vision

How do grievers *get* a vision? We sometimes think about vision as something only great leaders or artists or philosophers have. But the secret is in the acceptance of change. If we have arrived at this phase, we have accepted that we, and our relationship with our loved one has changed. And that, in turn, has changed our perception of our world and of our future. The next step is envisioning the future we *want* – the future that will be fulfilling.

Grievers who are moving into Creation as a result of a loss do not ask, "What does this mean for me" but "How does this connect beyond me." They do not use themselves as a primary field of focus, but look to larger realities. This means that they no longer frame things in terms of either the one dead or in terms of themselves. When grievers have recovered both their sense of self and their abiding connection to what was and the other, then both those points of reference fade before larger realities. Such truly creative persons do not need to look back and establish themselves or others, but look ahead to suggesting visionary possibilities *without any worry about realization.*

Amy found her thoughts coming faster than she could act on them. She talked about the many options for action that she saw for her future. "I want to help parents and I want to help kids. I'm a good speaker. I learned how to make speeches in school – where to look in an audience, how to use different tones of voice – I see the powerful effect I have on people. People need to know there is something they can do when this kind of death happens. They need to know it's ok to talk about it and cry about it, and that by making their baby real for them they can go on to grieve and heal."

It is in the vision, not the manifestation. So, anything acted upon is done so for its own sake, not for what it can provide to us or even how it can be expressive of our lost loved one's life or spirit. Paradoxically, although we're not focusing on our loved one's life, it is only when this point is reached that we truly embody the *meaning* of our loved one's life; for it is only at this point that there is no distortion of that meaning through the lens of our own need. We are not focusing on ourselves, nor our perception of who our loved one was, but on how to manifest in the future what we value about what we've learned.

George spoke about how much more connected he felt to his neighborhood and the people who lived there. "I want to run for a position on the board of my neighborhood homeowners association," he said. "I want to really make a difference in the way it's run and improve life for people. I'm pretty good at communicating new ideas." I remarked that he seemed to be comfortable now with being in positions of authority, whereas before he saw his parents in that role. He agreed. "I hadn't thought of that," he said, "but I know they'd be proud of me . . . especially my mom."

This is not necessarily an easy place to be. There can be anxiety involved in suggesting visionary possibilities while being in an unfamiliar role, to others who have never thought of or allowed for them before. We can be met with distrust, surprise, dislike, polite tolerance, rejection, fear, and even anger. We also may find that we can have a transformative effect on those who are receptive. But we may find it essential to prepare ourselves well, do our homework and research, and get our mainstream connections and credentials in order to be taken seriously.

Those whose path through grief has taken a spiritual direction may find that organized religion and its dogma no longer provide them with meaning. Their vision often shows them a glimpse of something larger and more universal than any one religion can contain. When we have learned to connect to others on the basis of universal experiences such as loss and hope and dreams, and on the basis of universal values such as connections and love and trust, we find that these are ways of connecting that embrace many differences.

Emily said, "It has been several years since I have been actively involved with organized religion. I wish I could be and I keep searching for a church I can feel comfortable in, but so far I cannot. I struggle to find a religion that doesn't want to just hand out platitudes. So for now I just stick with God and my friends and it works for me.

"I strongly agree with a friend of mine who said 'death brings us closer to our soul and spirituality.' I am finding this to be very true. I have had many profound experiences with my daughter's soul since she was taken from this earth."

Selene said, "I believe we create a new person of ourselves having experienced the passing of a loved one. We tend to go through this process of sorting out all the nonsense we used to think important and get in touch with what the essence of our spirit is. I found me in the experience of my loss of my mom. I know that, for my family, we each found out a part of who we are with our self and with her as a living guide with us.

"I went about learning my Reiki and had no intention of doing anything with it except on myself and family, until one day I felt so strongly that I heard my mom express to share it. I was sitting in her chair in my home and I could not get out of my mind the idea to simply be ready to teach. It bothered me so that I got my paperwork in order and spoke out loud, 'Ok, Mom, if I am meant to teach then I'll make a dozen copies of this manual and trust that you and I work together to expand people's minds to the love that is available in the universe.' I was shocked to have two people approach me in the same week asking me to teach them Reiki. I said 'yes' and I swear I heard her laugh.

"I have found through the process of grief tremendous opportunities for success on each level of life: physical, mental, emotional, spiritual. Those things that we held back seem so insignificant and so silly as to carry them forward into our newfound awareness of who we are."

A common experience of at this step is to perceive ourselves as having a greater acceptance of different viewpoints and a tendency to focus more on the positive attributes of people than on the negative. For these reasons we often express a sense of being "older" (this is a particularly common experience for adolescents and young adults) or "different" or even "weird" in comparison with our peers. It usually comes as an extraordinary sense of relief and elation when we who are at this point discover one another and realize we are not alone. The Internet – which is the most inclusive technological medium we have so far – has become one source of connection for people who have felt isolated in this way, and can be an extremely healing resource.

Griever's Toolbox:

★ Be aware that you are now truly embodying the meaning of your loved one's life.

★ Engage in the Values Clarification exercise (see Appendix A).

★ Fantasize about the future (what do you daydream about, what have you always wanted to do but never did, what comes to mind when someone asks, "What's your fantasy?")

★ Continue exploring spirituality and the deeper meanings of your grief journey.

Counseling Interventions:

★ Listen for an increased focus on the future, relative to the past. The griever is at this step when he seems excited about the possibilities ahead. This does not mean that the pain of loss disappears entirely – only that there is a decreased focus on the lost loved one and an increase of energy directed toward the future.

★ When the griever has a vision for the future, do not convey the perception that it will be easily achieved. Prepare the griever to expect to work hard for what he wants to achieve. If appropriate, suggest educational or training programs.

★ Connect with others who are on a similar journey. This can be effectively done via the Internet.

Chapter 23
Expression and Mistakes

Grievers who have not found a safe place to express their vision may learn to keep quiet, and take the risk of eventually repressing and denying their vision for the sake of maintaining a sense of belonging with others and/or to avoid a sense of personal failure. This can lead to getting stuck in the process, and is particularly poignant at this phase, which is so close to that of Fulfillment. But for many of us, the acceptance of our loss, ourselves, and life leads to the courage to try new ways of expressing our vision – which also means the courage to make mistakes.

In an abundant universe and multidimensional process, mistakes are not failures. They are instead steps that can lead toward fulfillment in the future. We who have learned to trust the process that has led us to this phase are no longer afraid of or judgmental about our own mistakes. Each one becomes a point for learning and growth, and a "no" can as readily lead to progress as a "yes" as long as we are willing to continue moving forward. In fact, mistakes can be the foundation for subsequent successes. Learning what does not work for us – in any situation or life experience – is inherent in learning what does work.

Professional counselors learn how to empathize with a client, and that involves the ability to not take personally a client's "no" response to our perception of their thoughts or feelings. If we can use that "no" as a doorway to a more accurate understanding, then we can learn from it. If we take that "no" to mean a failure on our part to understand, we stop expressing our perceptions and become discouraged. The same holds true for any mistakes.

Learning from mistakes involves taking personal responsibility for those mistakes. We can't learn if we don't see the mistakes as our own and blame others or circumstances. And when we understand that the only thing we can control is our own actions and reactions, then we can take responsibility and stop being victims of life.

Western culture teaches us that mistakes and failures are shameful things. We're taught in school, in our families, or at work to feel guilty about failure and to do whatever we can to avoid or correct mistakes. Of course, being human, mistakes are inevitable and that's why many people give up on their vision of the future. They equate failure with *being* a failure.

When we're afraid of making mistakes, it can be scary to take risks. We feel safer when we follow established patterns and rules, but that can't get us to the establishment of new patterns. Most of us make the same mistakes over and over again because we cannot see any other options. So, part of the Creation stage is widening our horizons to include a more expansive range of options.

We cannot move to Fulfillment without wandering down a few wrong turns. And so, if we do not allow change, how will we know a good turn from a wrong one. Maybe what *is* is the wrong one, and the change gets us back on track. Here is a side thought some may find astonishing, meaningful, or even disturbing: Although it is natural to feel that our life was "normal" before the death, because afterwards we are forced to change in a way we would not have chosen, how do we know that our life *before* was not the mistake – that, since we were not headed toward fulfillment that way, the change was a necessary and beneficial, though extraordinarily painful, course correction?

So expression involves risk, along with the willingness to suspend judgment and the ability to see progress in terms of infinitely small steps rather than immediate and obvious success. Any artist knows that an exercise can be done with some assurance of success once a certain skill is mastered, but a masterpiece is rarely produced without some trial and error or with any certainty that the result will be perfect or meet with the approval of others.

Amy read something in the newspaper about

parental grief that both upset and inspired her, and she decided to write a letter about it and send it to the editor and some columnists. It was the first time she had ever spoken publicly about her own experience, and she was anxious about the response. Her letter was published by the editor, but extensively edited. She was angry and disappointed, but finally accepted it and learned from how it was edited. She then expressed a desire to write a pamphlet for the grieving parents of a baby who was stillborn or died shortly after birth.

Expression also involves a conscious choice. While the acceptance of change and vision gives us access to the raw materials of Creation, it is up to us to make the choice to shape those raw materials into something that is capable of bringing fulfillment. And it is only by making that conscious choice that we will be able to see the meaning we have found through the loss of our loved one manifested in reality. And the expression of that meaning will be as unique as the relationship.

It might be helpful to remember that making that conscious choice does not mean the same thing as "trying really hard." Once the direction is chosen, once the first step toward expression of a vision is tentatively or wholeheartedly taken, that very action will change our perception and open another door. As Joseph Campbell so eloquently said, "If you follow your bliss, doors will open for you that wouldn't have opened for anyone else." All relationship is a two-way street, and our relationship with the universe is no exception. So, conversely, if no choice is made all the doors will disappear. The meaning lies in the process of choosing, not in the content of the choice. Leonardo expressed it well when he said:

"I have learned that life's greatest blessings often come in disguise. The greatest pain I have ever experienced has opened more doors within me and around me that I ever imagined to exist. I have learned that by facing and embracing my deepest, darkest agonies I have found peace, inner knowing, self-confidence and fountains of love that I had never discovered before. And, while I would never wish the agony of widowhood and loss that I have been through on anyone; the truth is that we all face challenges, obstacles, pains, and losses on our paths through life. And each of these challenges presents us new opportunities."

Griever's Toolbox:

★ Find stories about famous people and how they made many mistakes before fulfilling their vision.

★ View the film *Babette's Feast* and write about the themes of abundance, apparent mistakes, and risk-taking.

★ Use this metaphor: You are in a room. The room has a door, but if you remain there, all you see is a closed door. When you make the choice to open that door, other rooms with other doors will become visible.

Counseling Interventions:

★ Talk about taking risks and making mistakes. Educate the griever about the learning process, and particularly about how learning is impossible without making mistakes.

★ Emphasize the value of making conscious choices.

Chapter 24
Production

The process of choosing is a process of focusing, and it is focus which gives substance to the theoretical framework called *possibility*. That substance is Production.

By Production I do not mean to imply a finished product, but a productive direction that connects our experience to the external world. For example, production can take the form of applying to a school to complete a degree program, learning a new skill, visiting a career counselor to explore options for future occupations, adopting a child, planning a party, doing volunteer work, speaking on what has been learned to a civic organization, writing to a congressman about an issue of passionate concern, writing a story, connecting with a new group of friends, finding a new spiritual practice or church group or religious affiliation, traveling to a new place or in a new way, starting a new business, or any one of an infinite number of possible experiences.

Here is a little formula that I find helpful when thinking about production:

> *learnings and rememberings + strengths and abilities + values + vision + preferences = Production*

Production should express what we have learned through the grief process, who we are, what we value, what we are capable of doing, and what kind of world we want to see.

Mark's grief process had taught him to perceive life as a precious opportunity, and also gave him the faith in his own strength that made it possible for him to go against the mainstream conservative political climate in his state and initiate a program to provide free access to computers for lower-income people. He encountered many obstacles and red tape, and expected there would be more to come. He was also in the process of writing 2 novels that expressed his experience in different ways and images.

Chloe requested I administer a career assessment test so she could get a more concrete sense of the work she would be best suited for. Since she loved computers, I found a number of online tests she could take. After she took the tests we spent 3 sessions exploring possible career paths, and I began to hear her focus on what steps she would need to take. There was excitement and anticipation in her voice as she talked about becoming an architect, "putting a project together and building it from the bottom up." She talked eagerly about going back to school.

If the experience chosen expresses the meaning we have discovered through the grief process, then it will lead toward Fulfillment. And this focusing of energy often leads to a surprising side effect: issues that elicited strong emotions and reactions in the past seem to recede and lose their power. A metaphor I use for this is that of the camera: when we are focusing on one thing, other things fade into the background. This happens, too, when we widen our perspective. And we can also consciously use the camera technique to put problems into a different perspective.

Amy finished writing her pamphlet for grieving parents and had been showing it to people where she worked and getting a lot of positive feedback. She also sent a copy of it to her stepson's school principal, along with a letter asking to speak about it at a PTA meeting; a letter about it to Dear Abby and Ann Landers; and a copy to the editor of her local newspaper. She noted that the last time she had to drive her stepsons to their mother's house it did not bother her and make her feel anxious or angry the way it had in the past. Her perspective had widened. "I just want to be able to help one person," she said. "There's a reason I'm still here."

Each time we take this step of Production in a different way, we go back to Change, Vision, and Expression. It is an ever-cycling spiral of growth and motion. Each product that flows from the meaning we have found recycles us back to ground us anew so that our choices continue to have meaning. Otherwise, we are just choosing new things for the sake of choosing something new. That is not to say that even that type of choice cannot lead toward one more meaningful. The way the change process works is, more often than not, surprising; and choices should never be summarily rejected unless they involve negative or harmful actions. Here again, counselors must be careful not to judge products – or intended products – as long as they are positive and meaningful to their clients. And, more importantly, we should not judge ourselves!

There is another important caveat worth mentioning here as it relates to Production: It does not mean *remedy*. If we think we need to fix something, that is not the same as creating something. For example, a plane crashes or a teen shoots someone in a high school. The typical response of the media – and of many people – is to try to find out what went wrong so that they can fix it so it will never happen again. Does it happen again? Of course it does, because life events cannot be controlled. A focus on the opportunities for healing and connecting with those who have been injured or bereaved or traumatized by the event, or on creating programs to educate people about how to deal with loss and trauma, would be more likely to make meaning from the experience.

Be aware of the difference between control and creation, and steer away from focusing energies on the past (e.g., focusing on the circumstances of the death and investing energy in trying to make sure it does not happen to someone else). Creation focuses on the future; remedies focus on the past. Our strengths and abilities lead us toward enhancement; focusing on the negative leads us backwards as we try to do damage control and fix what is wrong. Our strengths are resources, and they can transform a bad situation into a good one. Filling a hole or building a hill takes the same amount of dirt, but the end result gives quite a different view.

Michelle was 15 when her father died. He had been her rock, her confidante, and her protector in a family system that was unstable due to the erratic and controlling behavior of her mother. Michelle took refuge in alcohol and was arrested and sent to me for counseling. She also was required to do community service work. Like her dad, she was a hard worker, responsible beyond her years, concerned with those less fortunate, and friendly; and when she began her community service she focused on contributing what she could rather than on the enforced circumstances or punishment that the work represented. She loved the work, and her supervisors at the community agency were so taken with her that they offered her the opportunity of a full-time job when she graduated from high school.

When we are focusing forward, knowing what is likely to be fulfilling for us will help us make the choices that will lead to fulfillment. The more information we have about ourselves, the more meaningful Production is likely to be. We use our values to point us in the right direction, and we use knowledge of our preferences and personal resources to help us access the raw materials we need in order to create the future we want. In energy terms, when that which is produced leads towards fulfillment, we will feel an increased energy flow. This does not mean that Production will become easy or feel automatically right, but that the energy spent to make it happen will be balanced by an influx of energy as it is created.

Griever's Toolbox:

★ If appropriate, go to a career counselor.

★ Use this metaphor: When you focus the lens of your camera on one thing, other things become blurred or fade into the background. Remind yourself how certain things that once were anxiety provoking or painful now seem much less important because you are focusing elsewhere.

★ Take the Myers-Briggs Type Indicator and other personality and career assessment tests online (see Appendix B).

Counseling Interventions:

★ Support whatever choices the griever makes in a productive direction.

★ Be aware of the difference between control and creation, and try to steer the griever away from focusing his energies on the past (e.g., focusing on the circumstances of the death and investing energy in trying to make sure it does not happen to someone else).

Chapter 25
Fulfillment

Fulfillment is the other side of Loss. It is the far shore of the river we could hope for but not see in the beginning of the process. It is the reward of Change. In terms of energy, it is what flows into the gaps made possible by what was lost; and it is also what would not have been possible without that loss. Although the recognition of that reality can be bittersweet and sometimes bring its own pain and regret, we feel whole and joyful, and possibilities are everywhere!

Amy was finding herself becoming a resource. People were beginning to ask her for her pamphlet, and a government organization asked her to do a presentation at a program on parental grief. "It makes me feel it's all been worthwhile," she said. "I think I came a long way. I'm proud of myself. I made myself a name. It doesn't justify what happened to me, but it makes it easier." She then said she was thinking about a career in counseling. "It's a big step," she said. "I can see myself talking in front of 1,000 people about this!"

When we hold on tightly to what we had and then lost, we feel we can keep it in some way. The reality is we fossilize it – it no longer is what it was, but becomes a hardened shell, a remnant, a moldy unused ingredient. What brought joy and delight and challenge and growth then, now brings only pain and sorrow and regret and nostalgia. In other words, in holding on we lose more than our loved one's physical presence. We lose who our loved one was as well. It is only by letting go that we can "have our cake and eat it, too." It is only by mixing the flour of our past relationship into the cake of the present and future that we can create meaning and fulfillment out of our loss. And it is only by mixing in that we retain the flavor and value of what we had.

At this point, we may look back and be unable to even recognize who we were before. We have been transformed through an oscillating, spiraling process of simultaneous letting go and moving forward – of loss and gain. Our energy level has risen back up to where it was before the loss – often even higher because we have learned how to use and control our energy. We have stopped focusing on our loss, on our loved one, on ourselves, and even on our relationship. We look toward the future with wonder, and remember the past with gratitude. Nothing is forgotten, and tears still surface on occasion, but our perception of the loss has shifted by the process of experiencing the new things that have become possible through change.

"I was much more fearful," Chloe said. "I was living in lots of fear and I've let a lot of it go. I'm not afraid of being alone anymore. I can see the difference between who I was a few years ago and who I am now . . . it's hard to remember how I was exactly. I don't want to go back. I can see everything so much clearer now. It's amazing. I just let it flow instead of forcing it out – forcing myself to do things that I don't want to do and cannot do no matter how hard I try, and trying to live up to other people's expectations. I trust myself now. And I don't blame my parents. I know they thought they were doing what was good for me. I've let go of trying to control my kids, too, and that was hard because I felt responsible for how they turned out.

"I see a big gap between who I was and am now." I asked her what the biggest difference was. "Being able to express the feelings that I have," she replied without a heartbeat's hesitation. "Before I didn't even know they were there. They were stuffed down. And I was always told none of my feelings meant anything . . . they were not valid. Now I know that's not true.

"It feels like waking up from a deep sleep. Now I know who I am."

"I'm not as afraid of change," Amy said, "and I'm looking forward to the future with hope."

"Loss of yourself is not the end result of grief, loss of fear is," said Selene. "We are faced with losing fear of death and embracing the ability to create and be who we are through the breaking down of the grief process. To me the Reconnection and the Creation processes are proof that we did not experience our grief without rewards to be gained by expression, by peeling off the layers of truth within us.

"We all like to say we did not ask for this experience to make us grow in this way, yet those that have experienced loss express only healing to others and have contributed to the health and well-being of all humanity in spite of their own personal pain. I reconnected with life upon my mom-in-law's passing, and with her in a million different ways – my teaching of Reiki, intuitive abilities I didn't feel before were acceptable to be shared. I began living a fuller life with her in it, her with me, and found even through meditation it is possible to hear the sound of love. I wouldn't be me, if it wasn't for her being in my life!"

From here, we move into the future with what persists, as we incorporate our relationship with our loved one and carry it with us in our hearts through all we do. All our relationships and experiences are part of who we are, but to grieve means to make a conscious effort to make meaning of our loss, and that effort makes the relationship with our loved one transformative in a way we seldom experience in our relationships with those who are living. Nevertheless, it's hard to overstate the value of including others as we make our way along the Grief Spiral. They give us validation that we're progressing, support, challenge, open up new possibilities and opportunities, tell us when we've slipped off track, and help us learn that our lives are parts of a larger whole -- a whole to which we can contribute something valuable and valued.

One of the indications that Fulfillment has been, or is being, found is when we become a reference point and resource for others. There will be a sense of wholeness; a sense of being ready for whatever comes next; a trust in self, and also a trust that meaning will be found in any future losses. This does not mean that loss will become easy. But fear of change, fear of death, fear of loss, and fear of failure will diminish – if not completely disappear. It is ultimately the process of *being* that brings Fulfillment, and the rest is detail.

Griever's Toolbox:

★ Celebrate! Do something to reward yourself.

Counseling Interventions:

★ Emphasize that this process can be generalized to any experience of loss and change, and make sure the griever understands what she did in order to get to this point.

★ Summarize for the griever what she has learned and accomplished through the grief process.

★ Be realistic and do not frame this as The End. It is a huge step forward, but life always offers other losses and changes.

★ Encourage the griever to rest for a while if she needs to, but not to stop the journey in order to avoid experiencing any more pain.

★ Celebrate your own accomplishment! You have helped the griever discover her new life – a life in which her loved one's presence is vital and alive.

Conclusion

Fulfillment will look different for each of us – as individual as we are and as individual as our relationship with our departed loved one is. Just as not all flowers need the same amount of watering, not all grievers will need the same nurturing or nourishing as we blossom into fulfillment. The concept of perfection is meaningless in terms of the grief process. To take someone else's progress as a measure for one's own, or to follow someone else's path, is to focus on doing it *right* instead of on doing it *well*. There is no right or wrong in this process, only that which is or is not meaningful. You cannot do it wrong and you cannot do it right. But you can do it only if *you* do it.

I believe that when we learn the lessons of loss, when we learn to live life on life's terms rather than on our own, then we have learned the fundamental lesson of human life.

I wish you well on your journey . . . and may it never end!

We shall not cease from exploration
And the end of all our exploring
Will be to arrive where we started
And know the place for the first time.

- T. S. Eliot

Epilogue

Spiritual Life Cannot Be Measured By A Physical Measure

– Leo Tolstoy

What our culture tells us

Robert Neimeyer describes culture as "an atmosphere, providing us with a sustaining communal repertory of interpretations, beliefs, and social roles" (2000, p. 113). This atmosphere is one we rarely question; existing within it is taken for granted as the baseline for normalcy. What it teaches us is as accepted as air and as automatic as breathing. But when there is a hole in that atmosphere, something about the way we function gets skewed as we attempt to compensate for, or circumnavigate, that hole. Like someone with a broken rib who compensates with shallow breathing that limits other aspects of physical functioning, we find a way to cope that can limit our psychological functioning. We deal with loss and grief in a shallow way because of a hole in the cultural atmosphere.

Where and what is that hole? Loss and grief are

experienced by 100% of the world's population, so why isn't it self-evident to all of us – after having had billions of people doing this for thousands of years – what to do? Our culture seems to have tried to deal with the grief process in a way that does not reflect what people actually experience. Rather than equip us with powerful, useful tools and concepts that would help us cope with the losses we all experience throughout our lifetimes, it has tried to treat grief as either a medical issue or as an issue that does not require addressing at all.

Few professionals specialize in or have a comprehensive knowledge of the grief process. There is a stunning dearth of research in this area proportional to its universality. The standards of the Council for Accreditation of Counseling and Related Educational Programs (CACREP) require no graduate course in issues of death, grief, or loss.

The criteria (V62.82) for bereavement in the *Diagnostic and Statistical Manual of Mental Disorders, Fourth Edition* (DSM-IV) draw an arbitrary line between so-called "normal grief" and a "major depressive episode" based on the amount of time during which symptoms are present (American Psychiatric Association, 2000). In addition, the DSM-IV does not include bereavement in its definition of a traumatic event despite the fact that they have many overlapping symptoms and can present as so similar that therapists have a hard time telling them apart.

The lack of understanding about so fundamental a facet of the human experience as loss is symptomatic of a cultural ambiguity about the grief process. On the one hand, we minimize or avoid it; on the other hand, we pathologize it. Our responses wander off into confusion and wander away into denial. Many of us profess that we can handle it alone, but handle what? If we do not understand the process we cannot answer that question with any clarity.

American society treats a death as a unique event that will never happen again, and seeks to deal with crisis only when one arises. Media coverage of deaths and disasters reflects this attitude by focusing on the specific details or symptoms (the particular tragic event, the tears of surviving families, preventability and legal responsibility, similar events in the past, etc.) instead of on the universal experience of loss, grief, and change. In schools and other institutions, fears about liability and who is to blame "can override other significant issues and paralyze efforts to respond to the crisis" (Cornell & Sheras, 1998).

The topic of death is generally considered taboo and our society does not accept grief as an organic growth process. Grievers often recount their efforts to teach friends and family how to relate to them. Loss is treated as a time-limited event, even though research has demonstrated that time alone does not heal all wounds and that, in fact, some wounds never heal.

Typically, as grievers we get support for a culturally acceptable period of time (approximately 3 to 6 months) and then are told that we need to get on with our lives as we had before the loss. Well-intentioned friends and family members decrease their level of support, sometimes because they believe it is no longer needed and sometimes because they fear that talking about the deceased loved one will make painful feelings resurface. As a consequence, grievers often feel isolated or misunderstood – or even abnormal.

Research shows that deficient social support is a factor in poor outcome of the grief process (Valentine, 1996). Complications develop when our attempts to express our feelings to others are met with inadequate responses, yet there is often considerable social pressure to *not* publicly express emotions that frighten other people – and also frighten us. Experiencing a variety of overwhelming symptoms without social validation, grievers invariably ask, "Am I crazy?"

The costs of short-circuiting or bypassing the grief process are staggering to society in the form of suicide, accidents, illnesses, criminal activity, and incapacitating major depression. The death of a spouse, particularly for men, is linked to depression, PTSD, and suicide. The death of a parent has been linked to both hospitalization for severe depression and a high suicide rate. And rather than seeing the reassuring outcome our culture encourages us to expect – a decrease in symptoms over time – studies show that grievers experience an *increased* rate of depression, suicide, smoking, alcohol drinking, illness, and medical hospitalization (Witztum & Roman, 2000). Ultimately, grief can lead to death.

In adolescents, symptoms of grief include a drop in grades along with difficulty in concentration and memorization, and a resultant lowering of self-confidence. Behavior may become disruptive or even violent, and accidents and illnesses more frequent. Withdrawal from school and social activities, apathy, lack of energy, increased attention seeking, anger, excessive guilt, and sadness are all symptomatic of grief. Males may initially react with aggressive antisocial behavior and females with self-injurious behavior, including sexual promiscuity. Approximately half of all bereaved adolescents experience disturbances in their relationships with both family members and peers (Tedeschi, 1996). Adolescents who have lost a parent, sibling, or friend to suicide are particularly at risk of suicidal ideation or attempts. And a symptom of having these symptoms is often a sense of being abnormal, and a fear of going crazy or being perceived by others as crazy.

Acting out can lead to criminal behavior and incarceration. According to Stevenson & Stevenson (1996):

> High school-age adolescents serving time for violent crimes in Bergen County, New Jersey, were five times more likely than other students to have lost a parent through death or abandonment before age 5. It is thought that unresolved childhood grief is a major source of their violent behavior (p. 242).

Another study showed that college students who had lost a parent during childhood "perceived themselves as more vulnerable to future losses than did the nonbereaved control group. Perceived vulnerability was identified in the study as a . . . predictor of adult anxiety and depression" (Witztum & Roman, 2000, p. 145).

Many adolescents turn to alcohol or drugs to medicate their pain. Addiction in both adults and adolescents is often the outcome of unresolved grief, and addictions counseling always involves dealing with multiple losses – including that of the substance.

Teachers, administrators, and even counselors are often apprehensive about talking to young people about death. We want to think of adolescence as a basically carefree time without the responsibilities of adulthood. Yet adolescents in our society "are considered to be at high risk for acute and chronic bereavement reactions" (Toubiana, Milgram, Strich, & Edelstein, 1988). And, of course, bereaved adolescents become adults.

When our culture tells us we must be self-sufficient, in control, and focused on others, it creates a dilemma for grievers and their friends and families. How can we be self-sufficient and require support? How can we be in control and unable to fix our own or another's pain? How can we focus on others when our pain is so intense that it demands all our attention? These conflicting cultural and social messages seem irreconcilable, and when we are confronted with a situation that asks us to act in apparently conflicting ways, we act ineffectively – or not at all. Death is something we cannot control and we feel helpless; we cannot make the death not happen, we cannot heal those we care about, and we feel inadequate to deal with our own fears of death or loss that often surface on hearing about someone else's. Progress is perceived as an absolute good in our culture; so when we experience a loss and get stuck in the past or sense ourselves unable to move forward, we feel dysfunctional – or even defective. So perhaps it's no wonder that the source of the difficulties we have with grief and loss is deeply embedded in our cultural norms.

Has our culture always had these difficulties? No, not

to the same extent. Victorian society had a very strict social code of rituals and rules of mourning. Death was not only acknowledged and grief openly expressed, but mourning was done publicly and for an extended period of time. When someone died, curtains were drawn, clocks were stopped at the time of death, and mirrors were covered. Funerals and the receptions afterwards were extremely elaborate. People dressed in black for varying lengths of time, depending on their relationship to the deceased. Mourning jewelry was worn, which often contained the loved one's picture and lock of hair. Black wreaths on doors signified to the world that someone had died. Death was a common theme in the nineteenth century. Certain images were used again and again to represent the frailty of human life. Draped urns, broken columns, weeping willows, and extinguished torches frequently appear as elements of tombstones, portraits, children's books, embroidered samplers, literature and poetry of the day.

Then came World War I and the influenza pandemic of 1918. Estimates are that anywhere from 9 to 16 million people were killed in WWI and 50 to 100 million people were killed by the pandemic worldwide. So, between 1914 and 1920, approximately 60 to over 100 million people were killed suddenly, traumatizing the survivors, just from those two world events. People stopped being able to mourn each death. They were personally overwhelmed, and also concerned that society would shut down and not be able to function unless they were able to minimize and repress their grief. And that is what they did, aided by the remarkable breakthroughs in the science of medicine and the rise of hospitals, which removed the ill and dying from their families and neighbors. We are still dealing with aftereffects of those events, and of World War II as well – not only in the way we grieve, but also in the way we perceive life.

I find it interesting that many of us are more able to deal with loss when it occurs on a national or global scale. The death of a celebrity or esteemed leader often elicits an outpouring of grief that on the surface seems all out of proportion to our actual personal connection to the deceased. The death of someone known by a multitude becomes an acceptable channel for our own pain – one through which we can share openly, receiving the support and validation we crave without risking rejection or denial. When everyone seems to be feeling the same pain, we feel safe in expressing our own. Conversely, when everyone is traumatized and confused about how to express their feelings; when we are encouraged by society to focus on fear, anger, and blame – as Americans have been since September 11, 2001 – everyone runs the risk of getting stuck in the grief process. People often say, "9/11 changed everything." But instead of using that change constructively, many have allowed themselves to become its victims.

In a world where death and loss is a normal part of life, American culture faces a challenge. We need to educate ourselves and our children, and then demand that our communities and schools and workplaces and churches become accurate and helpful resources for grievers. When our culture does not educate us, we must educate our culture.

What the experts tell us

Our society's perspective on mental health is rooted in the medical model. The study of loss has been approached in much the same way as has the study of illness (Attig, 2004). Consequently, most mental health professionals focus on the symptoms of loss as the problems – which is analogous to saying the bleeding is the problem, not the wound. Anxiety, depression, anger, substance abuse, delinquency or ADHD in children, spiritual visions, suicidal ideation, disorientation to reality, and PTSD are symptoms of grief that are treated as discrete pathologies.

Research continues to focus on symptoms, complications, and behaviors. When researchers focus on depression, for example, they focus on the nature of the symptom rather than its source. Profound sadness along with thoughts about death may be part of depression, but they are also symptoms of grief and loss. And while depression is treated as a disorder, grief and loss are normal indicators of living. Without knowing someone's loss history, we cannot tell whether the problem is clinical depression or normal grief.

We turn to our physicians first in times of crisis. Family physicians and general practitioners write more than 60% of the prescriptions for psychotropic medications (Buelow & Chafetz, 1996). The symptoms of grief are often responsive to those medications, and grievers are often medicated in a well-meaning attempt to help them return to a "normal" life as quickly as possible. Many of us are likely to cooperate and accept this view of our problems. Grief is intensely painful, and we are reluctant or afraid to allow the pain to take its course. When relief is readily available in pill form, its attraction is obvious – especially when approved by the respected and kindly family doctor and/or encouraged by concerned friends and family members (Rando, 1993). But when we are medicated, not only are symptoms diminished, but also the need for transformative change (Cordoba, Wilson, & Orten, 1983).

The symptoms of loss can also be viewed as distress signals. When we are in crisis, the symptoms warn us that change is necessary, and communicate that warning to others. If the behavior is seen as abnormal, the conduits to change may be blocked (Halleck, 1974).

Medication stabilizes the system and becomes the agent of the status quo. The disequilibrium we feel is balanced by the drug, and brings relief from the anxiety that arises from a short-circuited grief process. Moreover, when the long-term pain of grief leads to an attempt at avoidance through medication, we are vulnerable to addiction (Rando, 1993).

A recent study calls into serious question the effect of medication on grief. Reynolds, Pasternak, Frank, Perel, Cornes, Houck, Mazumdar, Dew & Kupfer (1999) conducted a 16-week study of 80 subjects, 50 years old and older, who had major depressive episodes within 6 months before or 12 months after the death of a spouse or significant other. They discovered that, while medication had an ameliorative effect on depression, it had no differential effect on the intensity of grief.

> There are at least two possible explanations for this phenomenon. The first is that depressive symptoms may represent biological dysregulation (e.g., sleep and appetite disturbances) more amenable to pharmacologic intervention, while persisting grief may represent unresolved problems of loss and difficulty in performing role transition tasks. Psychotherapy may

need to be longer and/or more specific to facilitate resolution of grief. A second possibility, however, is that persistence of grief is not necessarily abnormal or pathological. Preoccupation with the memory of the lost spouse might be the normal or necessary sequela of genuine attachment and part of a necessary sustenance of life.

Medication is beneficial – and even necessary – when there are coexisting conditions such as schizophrenia, bipolar disorder, anxiety disorder, adjustment disorder, brief reactive psychosis, physical illness, sleep deprivation, and major depression that is not resolving with psychotherapy (Buelow & Chafetz, 1996; Rando, 1993). It may also be warranted for a limited time when we are at risk for suicide or accidents (Hollister, 1972). These are factors that overwhelm our capacity to expend energy on working through feelings. But too often the physician or psychiatrist writing the prescription makes a quick assessment based on the relative evidence of a few symptoms. And their patients, believing that drugs are a "magic bullet," often put their faith in the pills and do not continue with psychotherapy. According to Rando (1993), "mourners are seduced into being promised relief by an agent that actually exacerbates distress" (p. 195).

A disturbing fact is that those who prescribe offer

more medication to women than to men (Rando, 1993). Another concern is the message implicit in prescribing medication for a griever. It is a message that says, "The expression of anguish, anger, or guilt is unacceptable or abnormal" – a message that itself can complicate the grief process.

These concerns seem especially relevant in our time with the omnipresence of managed care. Grief is a long-term redevelopmental process that often requires care and support for years. That is not viewed as practical or even feasible under a managed care plan with 6- or 10-session limits.

Most experts on grief – those who have given us the theories that have become culturally accepted frameworks – have come from a medical background. Classical theories of grief have told us that we need to experience our feelings, accept the loss, adjust to our new reality, give up our lost relationship, and transfer our feelings to new relationships. The theories tend to focus on a balance achieved within a context that remains the same except for the absence of the loved one, rather than a change in both us *and* our environment. They tell us that recovery is the absence of pain, or that it is "reinvesting in life."

Those who adhere to psychodynamic and Freudian theories especially, tell us that if we do not – or cannot – follow their prescription to renounce our connection to our lost loved one, we will suffer and be perceived as pathological. On the other hand, "It is not clear, from an empirical point of view, how many people actually relinquish their relationship with the deceased. Many people seem to hold on to the relationship and they do not necessarily suffer from adverse influences" (Brom & Kleber, 2000, p. 51). This is a clear example of the disconnect between medically based theory and the actual experience of grievers.

Attig (2004) sums up the problems inherent in the medical model this way:

> Thinking of grieving in medical terms (construing bereavement as analogous to an illness or wound, grief reactions as symptoms, and grieving as healing or recovery) again suggests that grieving happens to us following bereavement, simply takes time, and is choiceless. Caregiving is a matter of treating symptoms . . . and medical models mischaracterize normal grieving as pathological. [Medical model and stage theories do not respect] the individuality of the bereaved — they urge that grievers are far more alike and predictable than they are, they misapply statistical generalizations to individual grievers, and they often lead adherents to impose

inappropriate expectations upon grievers. (p. 345).

Nearly everyone, even those with the most rudimentary understanding of the grief process, knows about Dr. Elisabeth Kübler-Ross's 5-stage theory (Denial, Anger, Bargaining, Depression, Acceptance). Her groundbreaking work defines the current cultural atmosphere of the grief process – even though her theory was constructed primarily with the dying, rather than the grieving, in mind (Kübler-Ross, 1969). Subsequent theorists stand on her shoulders, and all grievers have benefited from the way her theory normalizes their emotions and experiences. Yet there have been several theories of bereavement published that go beyond her final stage of Acceptance; that recognize the fact that, while acceptance may be a sufficient condition for one who is approaching the end of life, it is necessary but not sufficient for one whose life is continuing.

Although perceptions of the grief process are gradually changing within the tiny community of psychology professionals, there is a spacious time lag between the presentation of new theories and their assimilation into the popular culture. Most of us still think of the grief process as described by the traditional models: internal rather than relational, recuperative rather than transformative, comprised of hierarchical and sequential stages from which any deviation is pathological, requiring a disengagement from what has been lost, and ending within a limited time frame after which we will resume living happily and form new relationships. Most of us expect that when we suffer a loss, we will experience it in this way. The result is that most of us are unprepared for the reality of grief and view it from a perspective that often inhibits healing instead of facilitating it. The fact that grieving can be a positive growth experience is not part of this cultural atmosphere.

Fortunately for all of us, the atmosphere is changing. Hagman (2001) says:

> . . . the emphasis on relinquishment has so dominated the psychoanalytic perspective that normal processes of preservation and continuity have been neglected, if not pathologized . . . [I] have emphasized the transformation and internal restructuralization of the attachment to the deceased person (p. 21-22).

Russac, Steighner, and Canto (2002) put it this way:

> For 85 years the grief work model has constituted

"normal science" in the field of thanatology, focusing our attention on hyper-cathexis/decathexis at the expense of other important aspects of mourning. Many would argue that the time is ripe for a fundamental change in the way we conceptualize the mourning process (p. 465).

And more wisdom from Neimeyer (2000):

I cannot endorse the implication that a normative pattern of grieving can be prescriptive or diagnostic, and that deviations from such a course are to be considered "abnormal" or "pathological." More subtly, I would question whether emotional responses should be considered the primary focus of our grief theories, to the exclusion or minimization of behavior and meaning. And finally, I have doubts about the individualistic bias of traditional theories of bereavement, which tend to construe grief as an entirely private act, experienced outside the context of human relatedness (p. 85).

Theorists are moving closer to a process (as opposed to event or medical model) perspective. We seem to be arriving at a critical mass of professionals who say grievers need to recognize the continuity of their relationship with the deceased, realize that a "normal" process is a theme with many variations, and place greater significance on the context of the loss. Some are recognizing that grievers need to find a new identity and to focus energy on new things. And yet moving forward is generally described in terms of compensation rather than enhancement, and we know *beyond a doubt* that the grief process can result in tremendous enhancement. With few exceptions, those who have fully engaged in the grief process remark with surprise that they have become better in some way – not in spite of their loss, but *because* of their loss. So . . .

The transformative perspective

A crisis is often defined as a sudden, unexpected, or unpredictable event that creates inordinate stress on coping skills. Increasingly, however, those who study adult lifespan development have come to view a crisis – such as a profound loss – less as a disruption with the attendant goal of getting back to "normal," and more as an opportunity for development and a catalyst for growth. This perspective sees crisis as transformative, freeing us from old ways of organizing and perceiving the world; and allowing a redifferentiation, and the creation of new ways of relating to both self and others while integrating the past into the present. But in order for this to occur, both the self and the environment must allow for it. If either one does not allow for it, we get stuck and, unable to move either forward or backward, the process aborts and pathology results (Lieberman & Peskin, 1992).

The transformative perspective is a paradigm shift. It posits that grief is not an isolated event, a medical condition, or an illness that is responsive to a standardized treatment of its symptoms. Grief is the universal process of change, and our task is to make sense out of the experience, ourselves, others, and life within our changed context. We cannot deal with grief effectively unless both we and those around us accept that need for change. There is a growing recognition that the inability or reluctance of others to participate in grief can stunt, prolong, or sidetrack the process.

In counseling theory there has long been the awareness that some level of dissonance or imbalance must be created within a client or family system before change can occur. Changes that are imposed externally feel frightening or chaotic or disorienting; yet, without them, we must internally generate some degree of disorder or confusion in order to change.

The more recent theories of bereavement recognize that when a griever experiences confusion, anxiety, and profound sadness, those responses are not abnormal. They are the appropriate responses of someone who is striving to deal with a changed reality and relationships, and who is doing so not only internally but also within a social and cultural context on multidimensional levels. As Attig (2004) points out, "When we lose someone we care about or love, we experience our daily life pattern as undone. It can never be just as it was before the death (p. 347)."

Those who study bereavement are also becoming aware that when we do change as an outcome of a loss, we often perceive it as a positive change. Tedeschi & Calhoun (1995) state eloquently what many grievers discover for themselves:

> It is evident that religious, literary, and psychological descriptions of coping with crisis all contain elements of the idea that gains can be made beyond restoration of psychological and spiritual equilibrium as a result of engaging suffering, and that struggling through life crises may be the only route to wisdom and the highest form of living (pp. 12-13).

A focus on the positive aspects of change following loss can facilitate healing, and positive thoughts and feelings are normal components of the grief process. Frantz, Farrell & Trolley (2001) found that 84% of grievers reported positive outcomes following their loss. Davis (2001) discovered that between 75% and 90% reported benefits deriving from trauma and loss. Davis also notes that the extent to which grievers experience benefits has more to do with their subjective experience of an ordeal than with the specific nature of the ordeal itself.

Among the types of benefits most frequently reported by grievers are: a clearer sense of identity, a greater awareness of their own strength, self-esteem, self-confidence, assertiveness, enhanced relationships with family and friends, a heightened desire to connect with others, empathy with the suffering of others, priorities that reflect a deeper appreciation of life and less focus on material things, increased faith, a decreased tendency to be judgmental and an increased valuing of diversity, patience, a loss of the fear of death, and a loss of the fear of speaking their own truth. Milo (2001) says, "What was important in life became simpler, more basic, and incredibly clear, and trivial things could no longer bother or interest them" (p. 124).

In adolescence, the experience of loss can, and often does, lay the foundation for resilience. Adolescents report more empathy for others and deeper and more meaningful relationships. But the adolescent's grief is often misperceived as a developmental problem or as acting out (Hill & Foster, 1996). Ironically, whether the adolescent's ego development will be impeded or enhanced by a traumatic loss depends primarily on the availability of appropriate and effective adult support (Podell, 1989).

Along with benefit finding, meaning making is an integral part of the transformative process. If an event does not make sense, it is difficult to perceive the benefits that derive from it. Meaning making can give us a framework within which to deal with a loss, and also give us a framework within which to make sense of a reality that is fundamentally changed. In other words, meaning making begins to fill in the blanks and answer the *why* questions so that we can move toward recovery.

Meaning making is an active process, and it is, in fact, the activity of making choices that makes transformation possible:

> We stretch into inevitably new meanings. And we change ourselves in the process. Death, bereavement, and our grief reactions are not matters of choice. But grieving . . . as an active response to them is pervaded with choice. Grieving as response is not yet another matter of what happens to us but rather a matter of what we do with what happens to us. We must choose our own path in transforming the course of our lives following bereavement (Attig, 2004, p. 343-

344).

One way of thinking about the transformative process is comparing it to suddenly being transported to a foreign country. At first, everything is unfamiliar and feels confusing and disorienting. After awhile, you learn the streets, the resources, the shops, the culture, you make friends and find interests, and the place becomes comfortable and familiar. It becomes yours. As one of the characters in the movie *L'Auberge Espagnole* observes: "When you first arrive in a new city, nothing makes sense. Everything's unknown, virgin... After you've lived here, walked these streets, you'll know them inside out. You'll know these people. Once you've lived here, crossed this street 10, 20, 1000 times... it'll belong to you because you've lived there. That was about to happen to me, but I didn't know it yet."

One of the ways I visualize the transformative process is in terms of 2 intersecting circles:

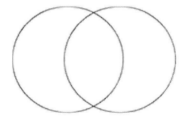

Circle #1 represents the previous reality, part of which is now missing; Circle #2 represents a future reality, part of which is unknown. The area where the circles intersect represents that which persists. The transformative process is the gradual spiraling movement from living in Circle #1 to accepting and learning to live in Circle #2. Meaning making can help us glimpse the contours of Circle #2, thus making the future seem less anxiety-provoking, more accessible, and more hopeful.

Traditional theories of bereavement have tended to minimize the fact that meaning making is singularly personal. As Rubin, Malkinson & Witztum (2000) put it, " . . . individuals respond to loss with infinite variety and complexity along a multitude of dimensions" (p. 30). How we perceive the changed reality we confront following a loss is less a matter of the objective facts of the reality itself and much more a matter of the significance of that reality for us. Likewise, what is considered "normal" and what is considered "pathological" with regard to any individual's grief process is not a matter of the specific loss or any psychological standards for measuring healthy coping, but a matter of the interaction between that individual's psyche, relationship to the one who died, and social and cultural context.

One question that emerges from the above perspective is, "Is there any role for the concept of pathology in describing the grief process?" Hagman (2001) has an insightful response:

> What therapists call "pathological responses" may be unsuccessful strategies to maintain meaning and preserve the attachment to the lost object. Treatment requires not relinquishment but an exploration of the continuing value of the attachment to the survivor, with a consequent reconstruction of the meaning of that person in the context of the survivor's ongoing life (p. 25).

Another question that arises is, "If the transformative grief process is so individual, and if there is no way to quantify what is or is not normal, can we know what facilitates healing?" And, thankfully for therapists, it turns out that we can – as long as we are willing to meet grievers on their own terms in their own contexts, and as long as we are willing to understand the process as a multidimensional spiral – which is the journey between Circle #1 and Circle #2 – rather than as linear. I will talk more about that when describing the theory of Transformative Bereavement.

One aid to healing is identity redevelopment, or re-formation. A traumatic loss changes how we see ourselves. We begin to question who we are. A wife who loses her husband no longer identifies herself as someone's wife; a child – even an adult child – who loses a parent no longer identifies himself as that person's child. A loss forces us to relinquish the roles we played in relation to a loved one and all the ways we collaborated in the dynamics of that relationship. Indeed, Davis (2001) suggests that when we cannot perceive any gains from our loss it is because we cannot let go of those aspects of our identity that were conditional on the existence of the relationship.

Another aid to healing is when we recognize what persists at the intersection of Circle #1 and Circle #2. Part of that recognition process is learning how to make the transition between the relationship as it was in the past and the relationship as it will be in the future; how to accept not forgetting and not wanting to forget, while simultaneously accepting that neither we nor the relationship will ever be the same. Attig (2001) expresses this beautifully:

> We reweave threads of caring, first woven into the fabrics of our lives while they lived, into new daily life patterns. We blend what they have given, and continue to give, into the life histories we reshape and redirect. And we join our changed and enduring connections with them with modified connections with our family, friends, the larger community, and God. In these ways,

we find and make ourselves whole again as individuals, families, and communities. We blend the found and the new into unprecedented life patterns and histories (pp. 51-52).

Klass (2001) describes the journey of parents who have lost a child. He points out that, living or dead, the child plays a role in the life of a family. The stories that family members tell about the deceased child reveal that role, and those stories can facilitate healing when others accept them as a representation of the child and a way to continue her role in relation to the world of the living. That role will not necessarily remain static. In the beginning of the process, the most vividly felt connection to the child is usually pain. Pain sometimes supersedes whatever else the child meant in the family's life. This is especially true with a miscarriage or stillbirth. When parents do not have an opportunity to know who the child was, they tend to identify the child's role in their life as pain and only pain. Paradoxically, many parents find their pain comforting because it makes them feel closer to their child.

When, and if, family members can let go of their pain – or perhaps it is more accurate to say, when they allow joyous and grateful memories to exist alongside it – they can begin to reintegrate the representation of the child into their lives. They often acknowledge the child as their healer and spiritual teacher. Milo (2001) points out that this can lead family members to continue working on their own personal growth or to continue the work they perceive their child as having started (e.g., advancing a cause they associate with the child's life or death). I suggest that these dynamics are not limited to bereaved families who have lost a child. They can be generalized to all types of loss. As Rubin, Malkinson & Witztum (2000) contend, "The way the deceased was apperceived in the past cannot continue to exist unchanged in the present without exacting great emotional cost on the bereaved" (p. 31). They go on to say:

> Focus on the development and continuing changes in the relationship to the deceased expand our view beyond mere adaptation following loss. We continue to relate and rework our connections to the significant others in our lives even after they die because the relationships remain meaningful and viable in the hearts of we the living (p. 32).

A heightened focus on spirituality and spiritual experiences are nearly universal following a death – although grievers are often self-consciously reluctant to mention them outside the counseling or support group setting. The transformative grief process is essentially a spiritual learning process because it deals with the journey from the known toward the unknown, toward change, and toward horizons we cannot see until we arrive. It engages us in mystery, uncertainty, mortality, the meaning of life and death, and our own limitations (Attig, 2004). It frequently involves us in questions about faith in ourselves, hope for the future, and belief in the grace of God and the universe. The journey may or may not take place within a religious framework. And this spiritual journey can help us find meaning, heal, and discover new facets of ourselves. Accordingly, one typical outcome of the grief process is a strengthened spiritual belief system.

Many grievers sense the continuing presence of a deceased loved one. Many see, hear, or feel the energy of one who is no longer physical. This often in occurs in dreams or in the relaxed state that is somewhere between sleep and waking. Some report being frightened by these experiences but others find them comforting, natural and a welcome aid to dealing with the loss:

> A great deal of solace was found in the belief that the relationship with the deceased partner continued in some way. This belief held the possibilities that the deceased partner could communicate his safety and continue to be active in the bereaved partner's life. It was felt that the

relationship was dynamic and could grow and change. The most common configuration of the new relationship placed the deceased partner in the position of mentor or guide (Richards, 2001, p. 179).

It is intriguing that the more shattering the loss experience, the more central role spiritual beliefs play in the grief process (Richards, 2001). Those beliefs facilitate the shift to the new reality that contains the deceased loved one spiritually, but not physically. They enable grievers to connect past and future realities, and to remain open to a future that might otherwise seem too agonizing to bear. And the effect seems to be a lasting one. Richards's (2001) study found that 3-4 years following their loss, 77% of participants described their spirituality as a wellspring of purpose, direction, meaning and identity – even though the need to explore it in order to heal was no longer present. Similar findings were reported in another study by Milo (2001). In addition, the grief process itself was perceived as a pivotal transformative experience: "As grief abated, the self emerged, transformed beyond previous sensibilities. With new sensibilities, the position of self in relation to other was redirected" (Richards, 2001, p. 185).

Tedeschi & Calhoun (1995) suggest that a

transformative outcome of the grief process occurs when grievers sense a positive change in their perception of self and/or world that brings new learnings, when those learnings enable them to find more effective and fulfilling ways of interacting with the world, when the present and future come to be seen as worthwhile, and when the loss is perceived as the catalyst of the transformation. "As a result, survivors of trauma perceive themselves as wiser and blessed, although this is paradoxically the result of loss or suffering" (pp. 87-88).

I will talk more later about the specific actions and techniques that can foster transformation, but they include: following a routine, talking, crying, expressing feelings, connecting to other family members, remembering good times, talking with those who knew the deceased, going to church, praying, traveling, exercising, going to counseling and/or support groups, doing things the deceased liked to do, shopping, taking especially good care of oneself, dreaming and talking with the deceased, volunteering to help others, journaling, creativity (writing, art, music, etc.), participating in learning and growth experiences (e.g., classes), reading, and spending time at the grave site.

It is not time that heals all wounds, but living in a way that promotes healing – living therapeutically. Sometimes the wounds do not heal. And whether or not the wounds heal, the aftershocks of a traumatic loss can last a lifetime.

Medical Model	Transformative Model
Loss is treated as an illness to be cured	Loss is treated as a change in both the individual and their social and cultural context
Focus on symptoms	Focus on source of the problem
Prolonged or severe symptoms treated as pathology	Individual differences recognized as normal responses to a reality that has been changed on multiple levels
Medication can relieve symptoms	Medication can complicate grief process and mask symptoms
Pain is to be avoided	Pain is an attendant of change
Stability is recovered when patient's level of pain decreases and new relationships are formed	Stability is recovered when individual learns how to navigate and find meaning in his/her new world
Letting go of the relationship to the loved one is healthy	Reconnecting to the loved one in a new way is healthy
The only thing that changes is the absence of the loved one	Everything changes

Get back to normal	Find the new normal
Loss is a disruption of what had been desirable	Loss can be the catalyst for positive change and growth
The grief process is a straight line from loss to healing	The grief process is a spiraling movement from Circle #1 to Circle #2
Loss is senseless and meaningless	We can find meaning, and even fulfillment, after a loss as we discover our changed world
Time heals all wounds	Living in an actively therapeutic way promotes healing
The bereaved are victims	The bereaved are choosers and co-creators

Elements of a useful theory

Given the facts, research, and perspectives reviewed above, how do we construct a theory that makes sense and facilitates recovery from grief? Theorists who came after Kübler-Ross have offered a number of models that point in a progressive direction.

Colin Murray Parkes and John Bowlby's (1970) classic 4-stage theory includes the recognition that a new way of relating to both the self and the deceased needs to be found, and that healing entails the development of new ways of navigating a world forever altered by the loss.

Worden (2002) suggests there are 4 tasks of grieving: 1. To accept the reality of the loss, 2. To experience the pain of grief – experiencing a variety of intense feelings and working them through, 3. To adjust to an environment in which the deceased is missing – struggling with the many changes resulting from the death, including the practical aspects of daily living and the effects upon the sense of self and perception of the world, and 4. To emotionally relocate the deceased and move on with life – acknowledging the value of the relationship with the deceased, yet allowing the griever to get on with life.

Therese Rando (1993) developed Six "R" Processes of Mourning, which correspond to 3 phases of grief. She notes that these phases and processes are nonlinear and, while typical, not invariant:

Avoidance Phase
1. Recognize the loss (acknowledge and understand the death)
Confrontation Phase
2. React to the separation (experience the pain and express all psychological responses to the loss, recognize and deal with secondary losses)
3. Recollect and reexperience the deceased and the relationship
4. Relinquish the old attachments to the deceased and former assumptive world
Accommodation Phase
5. Readjust to adapt to the new world without forgetting the old (deal with the changed world, develop a new relationship with the deceased, form a new identity)
6. Reinvest

"A General Model for Personal Growth Resulting from Trauma" is Tedeschi & Calhoun's (1995) complex feedback-loop model of the transformative process. The greatest significance of their model is, I believe, that it is based on the assumptions that 1. We can develop a model of how growth occurs, 2. The outcome of loss can be transformation, not simply a return to conditions before the loss, 3. It is the growth perceived subjectively by the one who has suffered a loss or trauma that transforms it from a negative into a positive event, and 4. Transformation is an outcome of the interaction between the changed individual, her support system, and new opportunities that are perceived in or offered by the environment. They also say that when we find we can deal with that which was previously perceived as "unmanageable, incomprehensible, or unmeaningful," the result is often "a sense of personal strength, a recognition that others can be helpful in ways not previously experienced, and an understanding of the vicissitudes of life" (pp.88-91).

Hagman suggests 5 primary tasks of the grief process: 1. Accepting the reality of the loss, 2. Expressing and learning to control grief, 3. Managing alterations in the external world, 4. Moving toward replacing the physical relationship with one that continues nonphysically, and 5. Recognizing that accompanying the changed relationship are changes in the griever's identity (Brom & Kleber, 2000).

Stroebe & Stroebe's Dual Process Model says there are 2 co-existing dimensions to healing that operate simultaneously: 1. Loss-oriented coping – the focus on dealing with the loss and its emotional impact; and 2. Restoration-oriented coping – the focus on functioning in the world without the deceased and learning to redevelop one's identity (Stroebe & Schut, 2001).

Neimeyer's (2001) prophetic voice proclaims: "… the time is ripe for the formulation of new models of grieving that can help integrate and give direction to current research and that carry fresher and more helpful implications for clinical practice." (p. 2).

As a constructivist, Neimeyer focuses on the infinite variations in grievers' responses and contrasts that approach with the culturally accepted view that most of us respond to loss in a similar way. To him, each griever's experience is unique and resists classification. An expert cannot presume to understand a griever's experience without having interacted with it, and must approach each client receptively and respectfully.

Neimeyer (2000) outlines a number of criteria for what he calls "a useful theory of grief":

- It would not assume that death and loss elicit uniform responses across cultures or contexts, and it would be flexible enough to allow for individual differences and for evolutionary changes in a griever's responses.
- It would regard grievers as participants in the grief process rather than victims of it.
- It would not presume to prescribe what is or is not normal grieving, and would allow for the consideration of multiple theoretical orientations within the

therapeutic relationship.

- It would be holistic and include cognitive, behavioral and physical symptoms as well as emotional ones.
- It would focus on a process of transformation rather than on one of restoration to a pre-loss equilibrium.
- It would address the reciprocal effects of the loss on the griever's environment and relationships.

My humble assertion is that the theory of Transformative Bereavement satisfies all of the above criteria . . . and more; that it encompasses and embraces all of the more recent models . . . and more; and that it represents a framework that is expansive and inclusive, while maintaining a structural integrity all its own.

Most other theories of the grief process are, to varying degrees, based on the medical model. They make a distinction between "normal" and "pathological" grief, use time as a measure, have a linear perspective, and use either Kübler-Ross's theory or a variation that is her theory dressed in a different configuration. For example, Rando (1984) proposes 3 phases of the grief process: Avoidance (similar to Kübler-Ross's Denial stage), Confrontation (similar to Kübler-Ross's Anger, Bargaining, and Depression stages), and Reestablishment (similar to Kübler-Ross's Acceptance stage). In her section on unresolved grief, Rando pathologizes the process when she includes symptoms that are normal but prolonged beyond the expected time for resolution of grief." If time does not heal, why assume an arbitrary time limit? This seems to be a holdover from the medical model. Transformative Bereavement explicitly incorporates Kübler-Ross's work and then expands it into the transformative paradigm.

Most other theories do not describe how or why we move from one stage or phase to the next; they just say that we do. Most present as discrete tasks or processes what are better described as elements of a multidimensional and nonlinear movement toward recovery. For example, Worden's (2002) task model does not provide a sense that there is continuous movement, but rather a series of assignments to be completed. Although this is not a stage model, the tasks are presented as being hierarchical, sequential, and invariant. He mentions that anxiety, anger, and guilt are part of the pain of loss, but does not explain why or how to deal with them. Transformative Bereavement is a gradient guide to the process, rather than a list of tasks, symptoms, or components. Most theories focus on the *what* and rarely address the *how*. Transformative Bereavement does both, and in a coherent way that professional counselors can integrate into their own approach.

Many well-respected theories (Bowlby & Parkes, 1970; Rando, 1984; Worden, 2002) tend to focus on a balance achieved within a context that remains the same except for the absence of the loved one. Transformative Bereavement focuses on a change in both the griever *and* the environment. When most other theorists speak of moving forward, it is generally described in terms of compensation rather than enhancement, and we know *beyond a doubt* that the grief process can result in tremendous enhancement. Transformative Bereavement focuses on how to move toward this enhancement. It views life as a whole, in which a single change can affect our perceptions in multiple dimensions (i.e., the loved one, the self, the world, and the future.)

Another aspect of the grief process that is shortchanged in some current theories is the spiritual. To use Worden (2002) again as an example, he minimizes the value of spirituality, and that attitude on the part of counselors has been recognized as being harmful to clients. He states that the hope for a spiritual reunion in the afterlife is a form of denial.

However, a heightened focus on spirituality and spiritual experiences is nearly universal following a death. The transformative grief process is essentially a spiritual learning process because it is a journey from the known toward the unknown, toward change, and toward a new world we cannot see until we get there. The process frequently evokes questions about our faith in ourselves, hope for the future, and beliefs about God and the universe. That journey may or may not take place within a religious context. Spirituality can help us find meaning, heal, and discover new facets of ourselves. Accordingly, one typical outcome of the grief process is a strengthened spiritual belief system.

The theory of Transformative Bereavement does not just talk about being nonlinear, it *is* nonlinear. Time does not limit the process, since the changes we experience affect, and can transform, our entire lives.

Grief is the recognition that we have to surrender to the past something we wish were in the present and future. The process of letting go of what cannot continue while coming to terms with a life that is forever different is the grief process. The grief process is the change process. Even positive changes involve loss.

The 4 stages of the theory of Transformative Bereavement – Loss, Return, Reconnection, Creation – are composed of an infinite number of small steps/phases/moods. When grievers identify with one stage, they and/or their counselors may feel they need to deal with all of the elements or components of that stage before moving on to the next. Actually, in most cases, that would be counterproductive because it is not the stages themselves – nor the order in which they are presented – that is important, but the *momentum*. The idea is to keep moving, not to attempt to control the movement. If we perceive ourselves as being stuck, we will become dysfunctional in an attempt to create the sensation of movement while not actually being required to move.

So, if a griever in the Return stage gets the urge to try out or think about what seems to belong to the Creation stage, then that is good and needs to be encouraged. Conversely, if a griever in the Creation stage needs to revisit a phase of the Return stage, that is good as well. As long as movement continues, it is okay.

It is the assurance and perception that progress is being made – no matter how little or in what direction – that will instill hope, trust, and faith in the process; in self; and in the counselor, if one is involved. Reaching a level of closure and sense of accomplishment at one stage, and then feeling inadequate to deal with issues of the next, will often elicit more of a sense of having regressed than will the process of revisiting issues from a previous stage with a different perspective that includes new learnings.

The grief process is not a straight line leading directly from Point A to Point B. It is more accurately defined and conceptualized as a spiral. Sometimes we move ahead only to find ourselves feeling we are regressing to an earlier stage, or to a point in the past that we thought we had dealt with or resolved. This is often confusing, and we wonder whether we have lost some ground or whether our forward progress has been blocked.

We become discouraged and disappointed in our apparent inability to cope with our own feelings and experiences.

What seems like regression is a normal part of the process, and sometimes we need to revisit the experiences of one stage – usually more than once – before we can let go and move on to the next. Sometimes we just need to go back and see that our emotional responses have changed before we can feel confident about proceeding in a new direction – or even see one. A friend of mine put it this way: "It's such a gradual process that it's almost impossible to describe it in stages. The lines are blurry and one tends to jump back and forth across any imaginary lines. I would say, of course, that the general movement is upward. But it's a lot like the stock market with its depressions, recessions, and the bull and the bear."

In addition, change releases a lot of energy and we cannot sustain a forward motion indefinitely. Change is a complex process, and when we resist it – as the vast majority of us do – it becomes more difficult and wearing. Imagine trying to swim across a wide river without stopping to float or tread water for a while! Sometimes going backwards just a little is a way to rest in familiar territory before going on to explore the unknown once again.

It can also be helpful to keep in mind that when we feel stuck or unable to deal with issues at a particular step, it may be time to shift focus for a while and take a break from hard emotional work. Energy needs replenishing, and what looks like being stuck may simply be exhaustion. Self-care needs to be the number one priority in grief work, for without sufficient energy to deal with change – or actually sufficient ability to *use and control* our energy – we will perceive the tasks of grief as overwhelming and impossible.

I believe it is also important to accept the reality that not everyone will reach the last step of Fulfillment. Things happen in steps, not all at once. So, a griever who has brilliantly navigated the Return stage (or the Separation step, Vision step, etc.) may discover her limits there. The point is that she will have done *her* steps. The focus needs to be on our own experience rather than on regrets for any lack of attainment of steps yet to come.

If grief is a process, it must be recognized that it is never *all and forever*. If what we do is what we need to do, disappointment is not an issue and the rest can be dealt with later.

When a griever, and/or his counselor, senses that he is not able to move beyond the midpoint of a particular stage, that does not necessarily imply resistance or regression. It is more likely to mean that it is time to move along to other important things like living and enjoying until it is time to engage in the process again, incorporating that which has been learned and remembered.

It is *all* a matter of perception.

Appendix A

Exercises and Handouts

Common Symptoms and Feelings of Grief

Feelings

sadness
loneliness
relief
disbelief
denial
anxiety
fear
jealousy
empathy
overwhelmed
anger
helplessness
numbness
irritability
hopelessness

confusion
loss of control
gratitude
over-protective
unsafe
guilt
fatigue
phobias
yearning
depression
frustration
isolated
rage
quick mood changes
emptiness
shock
panic
self-reproach
resentment
resistance
regrets
vulnerability
love
despair

Cognitive Thoughts

"Why me?"

"It's not real"

"I'll never get over this."

"I think I'm going crazy."

"I should have done more."

"I wish it would have been me."

"What's going to happen to me?"

"Why did he leave me?"

"I feel scared and lonely."

"Am I always going to feel like this?"

"I can't handle things."

"I can't concentrate."

"I'll never be normal again."

"I just want the pain to stop."

daydreaming

difficulty making decisions

strong need for nothing else to change

obsessive thoughts

disorientation

preoccupation with deceased's life

preoccupation with possibility of self/others dying and
  memories of previous losses

suicidal ideation

sense of lost one's presence

Physical Symptoms

headaches
weight gain/loss
shaking
tingling
pain
blurred vision
dizziness
lowered resistance to illness
numbness
heart palpitations
constipation
shortness of breath
experiencing symptoms of the deceased
menstruation changes
nausea
dry mouth
flare-ups of previous condition
  (i.e., hypertension, asthma, arthritis)
tightness in the throat
urinary frequency
empty arms (child loss)
weakness
sighing
startle easily

hypervigilance
chills
exhaustion
abdominal pain
restlessness
sweating
heaviness in the chest
fatigue

Behaviors

quick disposal of lost one's possessions
dreams/nightmares
substance use/abuse
acting out
change in sexual desire
changes in eating habits and appetite
treasuring objects
loss of interest in world events
loss of interest in social activities
withdrawal
avoidance of places/people/activities that are
   reminders of the deceased
crying
change in activities
sleep disturbance
assume mannerisms and traits of loved one
telling and remembering stories about loved one
searching for loved one
hyperactive
absent-mindedness
visiting places (cemetery)
loss of interest in work
difficulty concentrating/remembering
drop in grades

violence
promiscuity
afraid to be alone
staying too busy
lashing out at others
behaving differently
sleeping all the time
regressing to earlier times
leave tasks unfinished
try to minimize others' pain by not talking about the
    loss
detachment
distracted

Spirituality

anger at God
"why" questions
questioning faith
seeking comfort in faith
becoming a better person
heightened perceptions/sensory awareness
feeling lost
searching for meaning in the loss
faith development
spiritual seeking and development
openness to newness

Memorials and Rituals and Holidays

Memorials and rituals serve many meaningful and healing functions. They give grievers a way to externalize their grief so that not only can they see it made physical in the world, but so can others. That allows the grief to be shared with others in a way that puts the focus on the loved one rather than on the griever.

Memorials allow grievers to create something physical out of what is no longer physical. So a memorial can be a sort of embodiment – in a literal sense – of their loved one. And, because memorials are physical and tangible, they allow grievers to feel closer to their loved one when in that special place or time. Memorials and rituals can be ways of incorporating who their loved one was back into grievers' lives. They can become the foundation for new traditions on special occasions such as birthdays, anniversaries, and holidays. They teach grievers that all is not lost.

Memorials and rituals can be created out of elements that remind grievers of their loved one or of their relationship. These can include:

· evocative symbols
· animals
· music

- poetry
- favorite colors
- treasured objects
- flowers
- trees
- scents
- candles
- sayings
- photographs
- toys or hobbies
- foods
- special places

Here are some types of memorials that grievers have found especially meaningful:

Memorial Service

You can arrange this, but you might also ask a close friend of your loved one to help out. Invite your loved one's friends and family for an informal memorial celebration. Ask them to bring objects, photos, videos, letters, memories, and stories to share. Gather in a place that was meaningful to your loved one. Sit in a circle and ask everyone to share, as they feel moved to. Do not feel that you need to share. Allow yourself to listen, enjoy, and savor the experience of seeing your loved one through their eyes and words. Allow others to give you gifts and hugs.

Memorial Garden or Tree

Gardens and trees are wonderful memorials because they are living and organic. Dedicate a flower garden to your loved one. Plant flowers that were your loved one's favorite kinds or favorite colors, and/or that remind you of a place that was special to both of you. Place one or more of your loved one's (weather resistant) possessions in the garden, and add a memorial plaque with her name, dates, and a favorite saying.

Plant a special tree that can watch grow, reminding you that love can continue to create something that grows and lives on after death. Place a memorial plaque beneath the tree. Add a bench where you and others can sit and feel close to your loved one. Find out if you can do this at your loved one's church, school, or favorite place. Visit there on birthdays and anniversaries.

Newspaper Remembrance

Place a special poem, thought, and/or photo in the local newspaper in memory of your loved one's birthday or anniversary.

Birthday Party

Invite your family and/or friends and your loved one's friends, and have a special dinner and birthday cake. Ask everyone to share memories and photos. Set a place at the table for your loved one and put his picture or a beautiful candle there.

At the Cemetery

· Bring your friends and/or family to the cemetery on special dates. Give them a few moments alone with him.

· On birthdays: Take a cupcake with a candle and sing "Happy Birthday." Buy a small weatherproof gift to place on the head stone or plaque.

· On holidays: Bring a small Christmas tree or other holiday symbol. Bring appropriate items for Halloween, Easter, Valentine's Day, New Year's Eve, the first days of Spring, Summer, Autumn, and Winter, or any other days that are meaningful for you.

· On anniversaries: Bring a big balloon and fresh flowers.

· If you notice a gravesite that is bare and looks neglected, "adopt" it and put a silk flower or other small token on it.

Locket or Jewelry

Buy a special locket, engrave it with your loved one's

name or initials, and place a photo of her inside. Wear this all the time to keep your loved one close to your heart. You could also choose a piece of your loved one's jewelry and wear it all the time.

Web Site

Create a web site in memory of your loved one. Display your loved one's photo, and share the story of your relationship. Include meaningful poetry, photos, and memories, and a guestbook.

Holidays

· Buy a gift and/or card for your loved one and put it somewhere that is meaningful.

· Give gifts of your loved one's things to friends and family.

· Set a place at the table for your loved one.

· Light a candle and keep it lit all day.

Photo Collage

Make a collage of photos of your loved one at different ages and frame it in a special frame, or create a series in different frames and sizes.

Memory Box

Buy or make a special box. In it place photos, letters,

journals, souvenirs or collectibles, special pieces of clothing, music, recipes, a favorite toy, a baby blanket, baby book, hospital ID bracelet, school report cards, drawings, sympathy cards from the funeral, birth certificate, or any other appropriate mementos.

Memory Book

In a scrapbook, put photos that tell the story of your loved one's life. Include newspaper clippings, awards, tickets, cards, letters, or any other mementos that have meaning to you. Leave the memory book on your coffee table or other accessible place so that others can look at it, too.

Buy a Memorial Decoration or Light

Many hospitals have memorial trees during the holiday season. Buy a decoration or light in memory of your loved one. Also, hospices and churches often have memorial services during the holiday season that you can participate in.

Quilt

Make (or have someone else make) a quilt from your loved one's clothing.

Plaque

Your loved one had places that were special to her. You can continue her presence in those places by installing an engraved plaque with her photo on it.

Music

Make a CD of music that was special to your loved one. You can listen to it anywhere and feel you have part of the relationship there with you.

Balloon Release

Buy a bunch of helium balloons, attach notes and/or photos of your loved one to them, bring them to a special place, and release them. You can attach a note in a self-addressed, stamped envelope and see if you get it back!

Candles

Light a candle at mealtime, especially if you eat alone. Light a candle at any time you want to remember your loved one and feel his presence.

Use your imagination and you will find many other ways to make your loved one's presence real in an ongoing way, both for yourself and for others.

Dream Journal

Keeping a dream journal can be helpful. Dreams often give us messages in symbolic form about how and what we're doing, what effect others have on us, and possible directions to consider for the future. They help us become aware of aspects of our lives that we may not be fully conscious of. And because during dreams we are less defensive and more open, they often bring us visitations from those we love who have died and are in spirit. In other words, they can open a window into our own soul and into other dimensions of existence.

Many people have difficulty remembering their dreams. Here are some techniques that might help you:

★ Go to sleep before you are completely exhausted. If you are overtired, you will sleep too deeply to be aware of dreaming.

★ Take a nap during the day if possible.

★ Don't wake up to an alarm clock.

★ As soon as you wake up, begin to write in your journal. Start at any point or image you remember from your dream and write down as much as you can.

★ Keep a special journal and writing instrument on your bedside table within easy reach.

★ Take 1-3 mg. melatonin before bedtime. Start with a

low dosage if you haven't tried it before.

★ Take calcium before bedtime.

★ Take at least 50 mg. vitamin B-6 before bedtime.

★ As you fall asleep, verbalize your intention to remember your dreams.

★ If you awaken in the middle of the night, write down your dream.

★ The REM cycle is 90 minutes. Try to sleep for a multiple of 90 minutes (e.g., 7 ½ or 9 hours is better than 8 for dream recall).

How to Help a Griever

Listen

This is one of my favorite sayings:

L I S T E N !
If you are having a conversation,
and you hear
two voices,
stop yours!

When someone we know experiences the death of a loved one, we want to help. We want to *do* something to make it better, or easier, for the griever. Don't try to make it better. Let go of the outcome. Each griever must find his own way.

We often underestimate the power of our physical presence and patient listening, but grievers often say that that is what they most appreciate. Remember, you can't take someone else's pain away, but you can let them know by your presence, your caring responses, and your hugs, that they are not alone.

Don't be afraid of silences or feel you need to fill them with well-meaning words.

At the beginning of the grief process, a griever may tell the story of the death over and over again. She is trying to come to terms with the reality of what happened. Listen patiently.

Be patient with tears and pain. Don't hand the griever a tissue that sends the message: "Stop crying."

Say the name of the person who died frequently. It's comforting to grievers and makes them feel their loved one is not forgotten.

Honor the Uniqueness of Grief

No two people experience the exact same grief process, just as no two people experience the exact same relationship. Things that were helpful for you may not be helpful for someone else. Offer specific, constructive suggestions, but never criticize the way someone else is dealing with their grief, think they're wrong because they don't do it the way you did, or tell them what they *should* do.

There is no time limit to the grief process, so give the griever whatever time she needs and let her proceed at her own pace. Don't urge the griever to give away the clothing and possessions of her loved one. She will do it when she's ready.

Be available for companionship and socializing, but allow the griever to say *no* when he feels the need to be alone.

Be aware that men and women often grieve differently. While women find it more helpful to express their grief in words and tears, men usually need something to do a project or activity. This is a generalization, of course, but it is often true and the source of much misunderstanding between family members who are grieving.

Offer Practical Help

We sometimes forget that someone who is grieving has little energy to focus on the everyday chores of physical life. Offer to make a meal, do laundry, answer the phone, provide transportation, mow the lawn, put gas in the car, pick the kids up from school, etc. And remember that this type of support is especially helpful throughout the first year of the grief process, not just in the first few days or weeks.

Don't say "Call me if you need anything." Grievers don't remember who said that, and don't have the energy to choose someone to do a particular task. Just do it.

Be at the Funeral

Grievers often remember who was there to offer love and comfort. If you knew the deceased and the format of the service permits, say a few words of remembrance. Stay after the funeral and be available.

Write a Condolence Letter

Your own caring words are much more important to a griever than the trite words of a greeting card. Grievers often keep cards and letters they've received and read them over and over again, so make yours meaningful. Talk about the person who died and share a memory you had with her or him. Use his or her name frequently.

Mention one of your own losses, and tell a story about how you dealt with it.

Be aware of the relationship, and be sensitive to ambiguous feelings on the part of the griever about the deceased.

Make a Note of Anniversaries

Holidays and anniversaries of the death can be times of intense grief. Be aware of when they are and call or send a card to the griever. Help the griever create new traditions, or a memorial service, ceremony, or place.

Talk About Your Losses

Grievers find it comforting to hear other people's

stories. It makes them feel less alone, and they often learn something from the way others have dealt with their losses. As long as you don't act the role of the *expert* and prescribe, sharing your experiences is an important service you can provide. Just remember not to dominate the conversation.

What to Say

What people say to grievers that is **not** helpful:
You're doing so well.
You should get out more (or less, or whatever).
Call me if you need anything.
Time heals all wounds.
Why don't you talk to _____ (someone else) about it.
I know exactly how you feel.
You'll get over it.
God never gives us more than we can handle.
S/He is in a better place.
Think of all you have to be thankful for.
Just be happy that s/he's not in pain anymore.
You're lucky that you can have another child.

What to say that **is** helpful:
How are you feeling?
I've been thinking about you. How is it going?
When my parent/spouse/child/friend died...

Tell me about it.

Tell me more. or *What else.*

How did that feel?

What do you think about that?

That's normal.

That must have hurt.

I don't know.

Tell me about the good times.

What did you learn from that/them?

I wonder if you felt/thought _____.

You've lost _____.

How did s/he die?

How did you find out that the person died? Who told you?

What was your immediate reaction after hearing about the death?

Did you see him/her after s/he died? What was that like?

Was there a funeral or memorial service? Did you attend? Did you have a role to play in it?

What parts of that were difficult? What parts were ok?

What memory of the person who has died makes you feel good?

What would you have liked to be different?

Movies

Movies are a great tool for learning, and give grievers the opportunity to distance themselves from their loss while identifying with characters' experiences. Some of these movies are primarily about grief following a death; others have a loss as part of the story but not as the main theme. Check the Internet or library for full descriptions.

(Not all are suitable for all ages. Use your discretion and view the movie before sharing it with children.)

About Schmidt (loss of wife)
Accidental Tourist, The (loss of child)
Always (loss of lover)
Annie (loss of parents)
Auntie Mame (loss of husband, father)
Babel (loss of mother)
Babette's Feast (loss of husband, father, lover, friend)
Barbarian Invasion (loss of father, friend)
Beaches (loss of friend)
Big Chill, The (loss of friend)
Big Fish (loss of father)
Braveheart (loss of father, wife)
Breakfast at Tiffany's (loss of brother)

Charlotte's Web (loss of friend)
Cherry Blossoms (loss of wife, mother)
Cold Mountain (loss of father)
Color Purple, The (loss of child, sister)
Crash (loss of brother, child)
Dead Poets Society (loss of friend, child)

Defending Your Life (afterlife)
E.T. (loss of friend, home)
Edge of Heaven, The (loss of child)
Eve's Bayou (loss of father, husband)
Ever After (loss of father)
Fanny (loss of lover)
Fearless (loss of child)
Field of Dreams (loss of father)
Fisher King, The (loss of wife)
Finding Neverland (loss of friend)
Fly Away Home (loss of mother)
Forrest Gump (loss of wife, mother)
Four Weddings and a Funeral (loss of friend)
Frequency (loss of father)
Fried Green Tomatoes (loss of friend)
Ghost (loss of husband, afterlife)
Gone With the Wind (loss of parents, husband, child)
Grapes of Wrath, The (loss of child)
Grass Harp, The (loss of parents)
Hamlet (loss of father)
Heaven Can Wait (death of friend, afterlife)
In America (loss of friend)
In the Bedroom (loss of child)
Iris (loss of wife)
It's a Wonderful Life (loss of father, child)
Joy Luck Club (loss of mother)

Junebug (loss of baby)
Last Orders (loss of friend)
Like Water for Chocolate (loss of mother)
Lion King, The (loss of father)
Little Women (loss of sister)
Map of the World, A (loss of child)
Millions (loss of mother)
Moonlight Mile (loss of child)
My Girl (loss of mother)
Mystic River (loss of child)
Officer and a Gentleman, An (death of friend)
One True Thing (loss of mother)
Ordinary People (loss of child, sibling)
Out of Africa (loss of lover)
Places in the Heart (loss of husband)
Planes, Trains, and Automobiles (loss of wife)
Ponette (loss of mother)
Rabbit Hole (loss of child)
Rumor of Angels, A (loss of mother, child, afterlife)
Shadowlands (loss of wife)
Shawshank Redemption, The (loss of wife)
Smoke Signals (loss of father)
Son's Room, The (loss of child)
Sophie's Choice (loss of child)
Spitfire Grill (loss of child, friend)
Stand By Me (loss of friend, brother)

Station Agent (loss of friend, child)

Steel Magnolias (loss of child)

Step Mom (loss of mother)

Sweet Hereafter, The (loss of child)

Terms of Endearment (loss of child)

Titanic (loss of lover)

To Kill a Mockingbird (loss of mother, wife)

Truly, Madly, Deeply (loss of lover, afterlife)

Ulee's Gold (loss of wife)

Used People (loss of child, husband)

West Side Story (loss of lover)

What Dreams May Come (loss of child, husband, afterlife)

World According to Garp, The (loss of child)

Wuthering Heights (loss of lover)

Y Tu Mama Tambien (loss of friend)

You Can Count on Me (loss of parents)

Safe Ways of Expressing Anger

1. Write about what makes you angry on a piece of paper, scrunch it up, and throw it into a wastebasket.
2. Hit something with a nerf-type bat.
3. Go bowling, and visualize what/who angers you as the pins.
4. Take some eggs into the woods, name them, and throw them against a tree.
5. Find a secluded or soundproof place or sit in a car with the windows closed and scream as loud as you can.
6. Punch a punching bag.
7. Pull tissues out of the box one by one very quickly and let them fall where they may.
8. Tear up a telephone book.
9. Walk or march with your fists clenched.
10. Dance
11. Yell into a pillow.
12. Sit or lie down on your bed and punch the mattress as hard as you can. Have a temper tantrum!

I Wish I Had... I Wish I Hadn't...

If only I had . . .

If only I hadn't . . .

It was my fault when . . .

I'm so sorry that . . .

I still cannot forgive him/her for . . .

What I feel most guilty about is . . .

If we had one more day together, I would . . .

Note: As you think about this, give yourself a reality check and think about what you can control and what you can't. How much power do you really have in a relationship, or over someone else's life or death.

My Support System

When we are grieving, a good support system is essential. Without support, the grief process is much more difficult and we are more likely to get stuck at some point. This list is meant to help you identify who is there for you and what things give you energy so that you can support yourself. Fill in the specifics.

People who care about me

friends:
family:
relatives:
neighbors:
coworkers:
counselor/mental health professional:
clergy member:

Interests that are important to me

associations/organizations/clubs:
church:
work:
sports/exercise/physical activity:

arts:
other:

Things that are important to me

pets:
special items of memorabilia:
special places:

Who/What I could add to this list to strengthen and expand my support system

1.
2.
3.
4.

Note: When a crisis occurs and your support system is insufficient or unavailable, call a crisis hotline such as The Help Line USA: 1-866-334-HELP (1-866-334-4357)

Grief Release Exercise

Do this exercise every day for 14 days:

1. Lie on a mat with your head pointing north.
2. Light 7 candles–1 white directly above your head, and 6 pink in a circle around you.
3. Meditate and pray, saying "I release you (name of loved one) because I love you. Neither shall grieve any longer, so that we might both be happy and go on to our new lives."
4. Then for 30 minutes (set a timer or alarm clock) talk and pray, and know that the grief is being released.
5. On the last day of the exercise, write his/her full name on a piece of his/her own paper and burn it with the white candle.

Note: You may want to think about how you will structure your 30-minute sessions, what you want to focus on, etc. It can be helpful to have a structure, but keep in mind that the structure may evolve and change as you move through this process.

Secondary Losses

When we experience a major loss, we lose much more than a beloved person. We lose a large part of our world as it was. In order to understand and begin to accept our world as it is now, we need to be able to name all that we lost when our loved one died.

1. Roles (spouse, partner, child, parent, grandparent, friend, sibling, companion, lover, teacher, student, protector, advisor, confidant, cook, repair person, financial provider, caregiver, etc.)
2. Activities (what did you do together)
3. Relationships (friends of your loved one, friends of both of you, other people who were involved in your relationship)
4. Expectations (plans for the future, hopes for the relationship)
5. Living patterns (ways of moving through the day, places, schedules, financial status, energy focus)
6. Physical sensations (touch, hearing, sight, smell, taste)
7. Trust in the world/others (what and who did you depend on to be stable, supportive, predictable)
8. Ideas about self/life

My Strengths

Think of this exercise in terms of *who you are*, not *what you do.* For example, if you think of yourself as a hard worker, consider what characteristics and abilities it takes to be one (e.g., responsible, competent, etc.). If you are an artist, think about what that takes (e.g., imaginative, graceful, etc.). Think in terms of adjectives, not nouns. Translate *doing* words into *being* words.

Even as a child, I was . . .
Everyone says I am . . .
I love to be . . .
My favorite aspect of myself is my . . .
In relationships, I'm . . .
When someone needs my help, I'm good at being . . .
When I'm going through a hard time, I can rely on my own . . .
I'm happiest when I'm being . . .
I have the potential to be more . . .

My Strengths (Adjectives)

Circle the adjectives you recognize as being part of who you are.

accepting
active
adaptable
adventurous
affable
affectionate
agreeable
ambitious
amiable
amicable
amusing
articulate
artistic
athletic
attractive
authentic
aware
brave
bright
broad-minded
calm
candid

capable
careful
caring
charitable
charming
communicative
compassionate
competent
conscientious
considerate
consistent
content
convivial
courageous
courteous
creative
curious
daring
decisive
dedicated
deliberate
dependable
determined
devoted
diligent
diplomatic

direct

discreet

dynamic

easygoing

eloquent

emotional

empathetic

empowering

energetic

enthusiastic

ethical

extroverted

exuberant

fair-minded

faithful

fearless

flexible

focused

forceful

forgiving

frank

friendly

fun-loving

funny

generous

gentle

genuine
good
gracious
gregarious
grounded
hard-working
helpful
honest
hopeful
humorous
imaginative
impartial
inclusive
independent
informative
insightful
inspired
intellectual
intelligent
introverted
intuitive
inventive
kind
loving
loyal
modest

moral

neat

nice

nurturing

open

optimistic

passionate

patient

peaceful

persistent

persuasive

pioneering

philosophical

placid

playful

plucky

polite

powerful

practical

pro-active

productive

professional

quiet

rational

receptive

reliable

religious
reserved
resourceful
respectful
responsible
romantic
self-confident
self-disciplined
self-motivated
sensible
sensitive
sensual
shy
sincere
smart
sociable
spiritual
spontaneous
straightforward
strong
successful
supportive
sweet
sympathetic
thoughtful
tidy

tough
unassuming
understanding
versatile
visionary
warm
well-informed
willing
wise
witty

Energy Focus

The purpose of this exercise is to determine where and how you focus your energy. When you understand where your energy is going, you will have a better understanding of where you are going. Follow the energy flow – it will lead you forward if you focus it forward!

For one week, keep track in writing of everything important that you do. Then, being honest, rate which of them have to do with *then* (i.e., the past), which have to do with *now* (i.e., present), and which have to do with *then* (i.e. the future). What does this seem to say to you? How does it feel? Is it constructive, constrictive, destructive?

This process should give you a good idea of where your energy is going, and where it is leading you. Put your energy into the future, and it will be there when you get there.

Then . . . Now

My priorities were . . .
What I most enjoyed doing was . . .
I used to think life was . . .
I used to be just like . . .
I tried to control . . .
I was afraid of . . .
I didn't trust . . .
I used to feel __ years old
I used to believe . . .
People said I was . . .
I used to see my future as being . . .

My priorities are . . .
What I most enjoy doing is . . .
I think life is . . .
I'm more like . . .
I have let go of trying to control . . .
I am no longer afraid of . . .
I have come to trust . . .
I now feel __ years old
I believe . . .
People say I am . . .
My future will be . . .

My Personal Ad in the
Surviving Death Gazette

About Me

Write 6 sentences, one each that addresses the following:

1. My family history (birth place, age, members of immediate family, etc.)
2. My interests, strengths, and talents
3. What others say about me
4. My loss history (deaths, divorce, moves, physical difficulties, life crises, etc.)
5. How I've grown and changed through my experiences
6. What I can offer to a relationship

What I Want

Think about who you are now. Write 6 sentences, one each that addresses the following:

1. What interests are important to me that someone else share

2. What strengths and talents do I want my new friend/partner to have?

3. What do I want to learn from someone else in a relationship?

4. What are my *growing edges* that need encouragement from someone else?

5. What are the values we should share?

6. Why do I want a relationship?

Note: The questions are intended to get you thinking in a certain direction. If any of them seem unimportant to you, feel free to skip them or substitute something more meaningful.

Assertive Communication

Assertive communication allows you to be fully who you are in a relationship, while at the same time allowing others to be fully who they are. If you want to get to know someone, you need to hear their honest and transparent thoughts and feelings. Conversely, if you want someone to get to know you, you need to communicate your thoughts and feelings honestly and transparently. If both parties in a relationship are not assertive, they will have problems understanding each other, are more likely to get angry and confused, and the relationship is less likely to be a positive and constructive experience.

There are 5 basic communication styles:

1.   **Passive:** I give in to what others want. I don't want to make waves or upset anyone. I don't express my thoughts or feelings. I'm afraid to say no. What I want and need doesn't matter as much as what others want and need.

2.   **Aggressive:** I say what I think and you're wrong if you think differently. I say what I feel and your feelings don't count. This is what I want and what you want doesn't matter. I can get you to do what I want by using my ability to intimidate you.

3.   **Passive-Aggressive:** I will tell you what you want to hear so I don't have to deal with your objections or criticism, but then I'll do what I want to do. I feel angry that I have to agree with you all the time. I don't do what I say I'll do or act the way you expect me to act.

4.   **Manipulative:** I can get what I want by making you feel guilty or obligated to me. I feel like a victim or martyr when I don't get what I want, and I want you to be responsible for taking care of my needs.

5.   **Assertive:** I tell you what I think, feel, want, and need in a direct and honest way. I take responsibility for myself and for effectively communicating with you so that you understand me. I respect your thoughts, feelings, wants, and needs, and I listen to you without getting defensive. I am myself in our relationship. WYSIWYG.

Positive . . . Negative

I always admired his/her . . .
I was not too crazy about . . .
Everyone said s/he was good at . . .
I loved his/her . . .
My favorite aspect of him/her is . . .
S/he made me angry when . . .
In our relationship, I was disappointed that . . .
When I needed him/her . . .
Sometimes it was hard to live with his/her . . .
I was happiest with her/him when . . .
The way in which I'd like to be more like her/him is . .
.

Types of Spiritual Practices

Personal

journaling
meditation
using prayer beads
fasting
therapy
going on retreat
chanting
creating sacred space
living simply
praying
keeping Sabbath
reflecting
grief
exploring spiritual websites

Communal

listening to a friend
volunteering in the community
saying "hello" to cashiers and clerks
random acts of kindness
giving change to the homeless
pledging to your congregation
being respectful of others
attending worship
caring for an ailing parent
taking time to meditate about family and friends
playing with children
hosting coffee hour
having dinner with friends
family dinner
tipping large

Cognitive

reflecting on the past week's sermon
teaching religious education
sacred reading
studying astrology
learning about the universe
studying mediumship
a book study

Physical

exercise
bath time with your kids
dancing
washing dishes
taking a bubble bath
camping
running
tai chi
yoga
cycling
recycling
nature walks
gardening
swimming
traveling
spending a day at a spa

Creative

painting
listening to music
needlepoint
going to an art museum
making pottery
writing haiku
playing an instrument
reading poetry
quilting
singing in the choir
writing a letter to a deceased loved one

Activist

peace vigils
multicultural work
writing letters to the
editor
working for social change
emailing your government representatives

Values Clarification and Action Plan

Values clarification is a process that can help make your actions congruent with your values, and in doing so, can make the result of your choices more in line with the direction you want your life to go. When we try to make choices based on a given situation, we can easily get confused by all the elements involved. But when we make choices based on what value we want to express in a given situation, the way becomes much clearer.

This exercise is designed to help you decide what terminal values you would most like to see manifested in the world. These represent ultimate goals, or what Milton Rokeach (the originator of the term *terminal values*) called "end states of existence." In other words, what do you want your world to look like? What is your vision of the future? While thinking about which 6 values you most want, ask yourself why you want them. Choose your top 6 values, then ask yourself which one you could be the poster child for.

A world at peace (free of war and conflict)

Family security (taking care of loved ones)

Freedom (independence, free choice)

Equality (brotherhood, equal opportunity for all)

Self-respect (self esteem)

Happiness (contentedness)

Wisdom (a mature understanding of life)

National security (protection from attack)

Salvation (saved, eternal life)

True friendship (close companionship)

A sense of accomplishment (a lasting contribution)

Inner harmony (freedom from inner conflict)

A comfortable life (a prosperous life)

Mature love (sexual and spiritual intimacy)

A world of beauty (beauty of nature and the arts)

Pleasure (an enjoyable leisurely life)

Social recognition (respect, admiration)

An exciting life (a stimulating active life)

Action Plan

It's important to do these steps in order (except for 1 and 2) and to not rush any of them.

1. While you're trying to decide what your core values are, keep these things in mind:

   – what direction your life has taken so far?
   – what value has been most important to you in making choices?
   – what value would you like to see be the most important in the world?
   – what value do others say you seem to naturally express?
   – which values can you let go of and not feel you're letting go of who you are?

2. Look at your top values and ask yourself: *Which of those do I think I have the greatest personal resources to effect?* In other words, what can you actually, practically, realistically, **do**? Which of your values **can** you manifest in the world. What talents, abilities, skills, knowledge do you possess? What are your personal assets? Make a list if you think that might help.

3. Wait, be patient, ponder, don't rush the decision-making process.

4. Choose action – what you will do. Match your talents to your values. How can you use what you have in order to do what you want?

5. Focus. When you know what you are doing and why and it matches your skills and you've thought about it, focus on it. Don't play the waterfront, don't spread yourself too thin. And watch the energy flow. When it looks like a shower, not a faucet, you are not focused. In other words, once you know what direction you need to go in, go there and don't get sidetracked by alluring scenery :)

6. Persevere, persevere, persevere ...

7. Conspire. Make connections. You don't have to do it all, nor should you expect others to do yours. In other words, you need to focus on what **you** do best and look for others who are doing similar things in different ways or different arenas. You don't have to go it alone but you have to do it yourself. Don't get upset by everything, but get upset by something. Remember that it is the sum total of all, and not just your own sum total, that counts.

8. Party!

Appendix B

Resources:

Books

Compassion Books:
<u>http://www.compassionbooks.com</u> The official book store of the Association for Death Education and Counseling. They sell books for children, adolescents, adults, and professionals. *The* place to look for books on death, grief, and loss!

Springer Publishing:
<u>http://www.springerpub.com</u> A health science publishing company, offering a section on the Psychology of Death and Bereavement:
http://www.springerpub.com/products/subjects/Psychology/Psychology-of-Death-and-Bereavement#.ULffoeTLTEw

Websites

American Association of Suicidology (AAS): http://www.suicidology.org Excellent information on suicide and its prevention.

American Counseling Association: http://www.counseling.org

American Psychological Association: http://www.apa.org The website has sections on Death & Dying and Trauma.

Association for Death Education and Counseling: http://www.adec.org ADEC is a multidisciplinary professional organization dedicated to promoting excellence in death education, bereavement counseling and care of the dying. Based on theory and quality research, ADEC provides information, support and resources to its multicultural membership and, through them, to the public.

Children with AIDS Project: http://www.aidskids.org Information and education about children with AIDS along with a variety of services for children affected by AIDS.

Compassion and Choices
http://www.compassionandchoices.org End of life issues.

The Connecticut Hospice:
http://www.hospice.com inaugurated hospice care in America in 1974. Since then, it has been the beacon and teacher of the growing hospice movement throughout the nation, and beyond.

The Dougy Center for Grieving Children:
http://www.GrievingChild.org This site provides helpful information and guidance about how to support grieving children and teens and their families.

Gift From Within:
http://www.giftfromwithin.org/html/articles.html
An international private, nonprofit organization dedicated to those who suffer post-traumatic stress disorder (PTSD), those at risk for PTSD, and those who care for traumatized individuals.

GriefNet:
http://griefnet.org A place where you can communicate with others via email support groups about

death, grief, and major loss, including life-threatening and chronic illness.

Growth House:

http://www.growthhouse.org With the goal of improving the quality of care for the dying, this site offers an extensive directory of Internet resources relating to life-threatening illness and end-of-life care.

Hospice Foundation of America:

http://www.hospicefoundation.org Excellent website of one of the best resources for the bereaved and terminally ill. I can't say enough good things about hospice. Most hospices have free bereavement support groups run by their professionals.

International Association of Near Death Studies:

(IANDS) http://www.iands.org

National Center for Death Education (NCDE):

http://www.mountida.edu/sp.cfm?pageid=307 An extensive thanatology library housed at Mount Ida College in Newton, MA . Also the site of The Thanatology Summer Institute and several online courses in the field.

National Center for Children Exposed to Violence:

http://www.nccev.org Mental health education

resource sponsored by the Yale Child Study Center.

National Public Radio:

The End of Life–Exploring Death in America: http://www.npr.org/programs/death Beginning in November 1998, National Public Radio broadcast regular programs in its series, "The End of Life: Exploring Death in America." At this site you can download transcripts of the original broadcasts, as well as resources, a bibliography, and readings. There is also a place to tell your own story and give feedback to the programmers. Among the topics covered in this series are palliative medicine at life's end, grief and bereavement, doctors and death, reincarnation and Tibetan Buddhism, and the biology of suicide.

National School Psychologist:

http://www.nasponline.org/resources/crisis_safety/index.aspx

Good, short, and complete information on many types of crisis situations.

Rising Sun Center for Loss & Renewal:

http://www.risingsuncenter.com Valuable resources for grieving children. Healing Hearts game is a powerful tool for helping children talk about their grief.

Sands Support Group page for parents experiencing miscarriage stillbirth, and neonatal death:
http://www.vicnet.net.au

SA\VE: Suicide Awareness \ Voices of Education:
http://www.save.org Provides education and information about suicide and suicide prevention, as well as outreach and grief support for those who have lost loved ones to suicide.

TAPS – Tragedy Assistance Program for Survivors:
http://www.taps.org TAPS is committed to providing support, care, and compassion to those affected by the loss of a loved one in the Armed Forces.

Online Career and Personality Tests

Career Assessment
Princeton Review Career Quiz:
http://www.princetonreview.com/cte/quiz/career_quiz1.asp

Career Interest Test:
http://www.livecareer.com/career-test
MAPP (Motivational Appraisal of Personal Potential):
http://www.assessment.com/MAPPMembers/Welcome.asp?Accnum=06-5329-000.00

Career Key:
http://www.careerkey.org/
Self-Directed Search:
http://www.self-directed-search.com/

Myers-Briggs Type Indicator and other MBTI-type Tests

Myers-Briggs Type Indicator (the original):
http://www.knowyourtype.com/

Socionics Type Assistant:
http://www.sociotype.com/tests/#The-Original-Socionics-Test

Jung Typology Test:
http://www.humanmetrics.com/cgi-win/JTypes1.htm

Keirsey Temperament Sorter:
http://www.keirsey.com/sorter/register.aspx

MBTI Discussion

Myers-Briggs Type Indicator Discussion
http://en.wikipedia.org/wiki/Myers-Briggs_Type_Indicator

TypeLogic (more discussion of M-B types):
http://typelogic.com/

Other Personality Tests

The Big Five Personality Test:
http://www.outofservice.com/bigfive/

RHETI (Riso-Hudson Enneagram Type Indicator):
http://www.enneagraminstitute.com/dis_sample_36.asp

Misc.

IQ Test:
http://www.iqtest.com/
Your Medieval Vocational Personality:
http://www.cmi-lmi.com/kingdomality.html

Locus of Control Test:
http://www.queendom.com/tests/access_page/index.
htm?idRegTest=704

References

American Psychiatric Association. (2000). *Diagnostic and statistical manual of mental disorders* (4th ed., text rev.). Washington, DC: Author.

Attig, T. (2001). Relearning the world: Making and finding meaning. In R. A. Neimeyer (Ed.), *Meaning reconstruction & the experience of loss* (pp. 33–54). Washington, DC: American Psychological Association.

Attig, T. (2004). Meanings of death seen through the lens of grieving. *Death Studies*, 28, 341–360.

Bowlby, J., & Parkes, C. M. (1970). Separation and loss. In E. J. Anthony & C. Koupernik (Eds.), *International yearbook of child psychiatry and allied professions*: Vol. 1 The child in his family (pp. 197–216). New York: Wiley.

Brom, D., & Kleber, R. J. (2000). On coping with trauma and coping with grief: Similarities and differences. In R. R. Malkinson, S. S. Rubin, & E. Witztum (Eds.), *Traumatic and nontraumatic loss and bereavement: Clinical theory and practice* (pp. 41–66). Madison, CT: International Universities Press/ Psychosocial Press.

Buelow, G. D., & Chafetz, M. D. (1996). Proposed ethical practice guidelines for clinical pharmacopsychology: Sharpening a new focus in psychology. *Professional Psychology: Research and Practice*, 27(1), 53–58.

Cordoba, O. A., Wilson, W., & Orten, J. D. (1983). Psychotropic medications for children. *Social Work*, 28(6), 448–453.

Cornell, D. G., & Sheras, P. L. (1998). Common errors in school crisis response: Learning from our mistakes. *Psychology in the Schools*, 35(3), 297–307.

Davis, C. G. (2001). The tormented and the transformed: Understanding responses to loss and trauma. In R. A. Neimeyer (Ed.), *Meaning reconstruction & the experience of loss* (pp. 137–156). Washington, DC: American Psychological Association.

Frantz, T. T., Farrell, M. M., & Trolley, B. C. (2001). Positive outcomes of losing a loved one. In R. A. Neimeyer (Ed.), *Meaning reconstruction & the experience of loss* (pp. 191–212). Washington, DC: American Psychological Association.

Hagman, G. (2001). Beyond decathexis: Toward a new psychoanalytic understanding and treatment of mourning. In R. A. Neimeyer (Ed.), *Meaning reconstruction & the experience of loss* (pp. 13–31). Washington, DC: American Psychological Association.

Halleck, S. L. (1974). Legal and ethical aspects of behavior control. *The American Journal of Psychiatry*, 131(4), 381–385.

Hill, D. C., & Foster, Y. M. (1996). Postvention with early and middle adolescents. In C. A. Corr & D. E. Balk (Eds.), Handbook of adolescent death and bereavement (pp. 250–272). New York: Springer Publishing Company.

Hollister, L. E. (1972). Psychotherapeutic drugs in the dying and bereaved. *Journal of Thanatology*, 2 (1–2, Winter-Spring), 623–629.

Klass, D. (2001). The inner representation of the dead child in the psychic and social narratives of bereaved parents. In R.A. Neimeyer (Ed.), *Meaning reconstruction and the experience of loss* (pp. 77–94). Washington, DC: American Psychological Association.

Kübler-Ross, E. (1969). *On death and dying.* New

York: Macmillan.

Lieberman, M. A., & Peskin, H. (1992). Adult life crises. In J. E. Birren, R. B. Sloane, & G. D. Cohen (Eds.), *Handbook of mental health and aging* (pp. 119–143). San Diego, CA: Academic Press, Inc.

Milo, E. M. (2001). In R. A. Neimeyer (Ed.), *Meaning reconstruction & the experience of loss* Washington, DC: American Psychological Association.

Neimeyer, R. A. (2000). *Lessons of loss: A guide to coping.* Keystone Heights, FL: PsychoEducational Resources, Inc.

Neimeyer, R. A. (2001). Meaning reconstruction and loss. In R. A. Neimeyer (Ed.), *Meaning reconstruction & the experience of loss* (pp. 1–12). Washington, DC: American Psychological Association.

Patterson, P. R. (1972). The use and misuse of psychopharmaceuticals by the pediatrician in the care of the dying child and his family. *Journal of Thanatology,* 2(3-4), 838–842.

Perschy, M. K. (1997). *Helping teens work through*

grief. Washington, DC: Accelerated Development.

Podell, C. (1989). Adolescent mourning: The sudden death of a peer. *Clinical Social Work Journal*, 17(1), 64–78.

Rando, T. A. (1984). *Grief, Dying, and Death*. Champaign, IL: Research Press.

Rando, T. A. (1993). *Treatment of complicated mourning*. Champaign, IL: Research Press.

Reynolds III, C. F., Miller, M. D., Pasternak, R. E., Frank, E., Perel, J. M., Cornes, C., et al. (1999). Treatment of bereavement-related major depressive episodes in later life: A controlled study of acute and continuation treatment with nortriptyline and interpersonal psychotherapy. *American Journal of Psychiatry*, 156(2), 202–208.

Richards, T. A. (2001). Spiritual resources following a partner's death from AIDS. In R. A. Neimeyer (Ed.), *Meaning reconstruction & the experience of loss* (pp. 173–190). Washington, DC: American Psychological Association.

Rubin, S. S., Malkinson, R., & Witztum, E. (2000). Loss, bereavement, and trauma: An overview. In R. Malkinson, S. S. Rubin, & E. Witztum (Eds.), *Traumatic and nontraumatic loss and bereavement* (pp. 5–40). Madison, CT: Psychosocial Press.

Russac, R. J., Steighner, N. S., & Canto, A. I. (2002). Grief work versus continuing bonds: A call for paradigm integration or replacement? *Death Studies*, 26, 463–478.

Stevenson, R. G., & Stevenson, E. P. (1996). Adolescents and education about death, dying, and bereavement. In C. A. Corr & D. E. Balk (Eds.), *Handbook of adolescent death and bereavement* (pp. 235–249). New York: Springer Publishing Company, Inc.

Stroebe, M. S., & Schut, H. (2001). Models of coping with bereavement: A review. In M. S. Stroebe, R. O. Hansson, W. Stroebe, & H. Schut (Eds.), *Handbook of Bereavement Research : Consequences, Coping, and Care* (pp. 89–118). Washington, DC: American Psychological Association.

Tedeschi, R. G. (1996). Support groups for bereaved adolescents. In C. A. Corr & D. E. Balk (Eds.), *Handbook of adolescent death and bereavement* (pp. 293–311). New

York: Springer Publishing Company, Inc.

Tedeschi, R. G., & Calhoun, L. G. (1995). *Trauma & transformation*. Thousand Oaks, CA: Sage Publications, Inc.

Toubiana, Y. H., Milgram, N. A., Strich, Y., & Edelstein, A. (1988). Crisis intervention in a school community disaster: Principles and practices. *Journal of Community Psychology*, 16(2), 228–240.

Valentine, L. (1996). Professional interventions to assist adolescents who are coping with death and bereavement. In C. A. Corr & D. E. Balk (Eds.), *Handbook of adolescent death and bereavement* (pp. 312–328). New York: Springer Publishing Company, Inc.

Witztum, E., & Roman, I. (2000). Psychotherapeutic intervention with complicated grief: Metaphor and leave-taking ritual with the bereaved. In R. Malkinson, S. S. Rubin, & E. Witztum (Eds.), *Traumatic and nontraumatic loss and bereavement* (pp. 143–172). Madison, CT: Psychosocial Press.

Worden, J. W. (2002). *Grief counseling and grief therapy: A handbook for the mental health practitioner*

(3rd ed.). New York: Springer Publishing Company.

The New
Atlantian Library

NewAtlantianLibrary.com or
AbsolutelyAmazingEbooks.com or
AA-eBooks.com

Made in the USA
San Bernardino, CA
30 September 2013